LANDMARKS & MONUMENTS
of
BATON ROUGE

HILDA S. KROUSEL, PHD

Charleston ‖ London

THE
History
PRESS

Published by The History Press
Charleston, SC 29403
www.historypress.net

First published 2012

Manufactured in the United States

ISBN 978.1.60949.640.1

Library of Congress CIP data applied for.

Notice: The information in this book is true and complete to the best of our knowledge. It is offered without guarantee on the part of the author or The History Press. The author and The History Press disclaim all liability in connection with the use of this book.

To Kohl, beloved grandson.

CONTENTS

CONTENTS

Acknowledgements

The author wishes to express her indebtedness to her husband, Walter, for his support and understanding, as well as to her three daughters, Marlene, Marie Antoinette and Elizabeth, for their unfailing encouragement and assistance during the planning of this book. A very special thanks goes to Elizabeth for her pertinent editorial comments and for sharing her knowledge of computer techniques to assemble the components of this work.

Her debt of gratitude extends to Melissa Eastin, archivist/librarian II, Baton Rouge Room, East Baton Rouge Parish Library, and to Charlene Bonnette, head librarian of Louisiana Collection and Preservation, State Library of Louisiana, for their invaluable assistance in finding primary source materials.

INTRODUCTION

Throughout the ages, mankind and the various nation-states that it has formed have attempted to define themselves and their respective civilizations by the monuments and historical markers they erected. For example, there are the pyramids in Egypt, the Acropolis in Greece, the Coliseum in Rome and the Arc de Triomphe in Paris, to name a few.

Cities, as they developed, followed the examples set by the nation-states. Baton Rouge, the capital city of the state of Louisiana, United States of America, in its time span has erected and accumulated an array of varied historical and unique monuments and markers that date from the early 1800s to the 1980s. Baton Rouge was initially referred to as the Red Stick (see Appendix I), which is what the Indians used to separate and possibly mark the territorial hunting grounds of the Bayagoula (or Bayougoula) and Houma Indians. Later, this is what they called the settlement that developed on that piece of ground. The French, in turn, translated the name to Baton Rouge. The variations in the names given to the nascent municipality are the first indication that the city is multilingual and multicultural.

Louisiana, first as a territory and later as a state, developed in a unique manner. Its geographic location was greatly responsible for this because the mighty Mississippi River runs through it on its way to emptying into the Gulf of Mexico. Control of the mouth of this river and its riverbanks became paramount to the European colonizing nations fighting for ownership and development of North America. From 1528, when Pánfilo Narvaez led a Spanish expedition that discovered the mouth of the Mississippi River, to 1699, when the French established a colony in Louisiana under Pierre Le

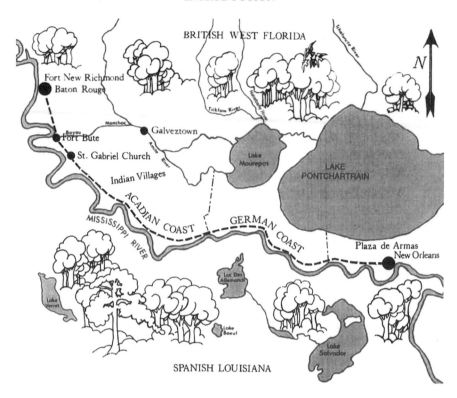

Scanned map of Spanish Louisiana. *Courtesy of the Baton Rouge Bicentennial Commission.*

Moyne Sieur d'Iberville, the area was also being encroached on by British settlers from the West Florida Territory. Thus, Louisiana's early history was part of the history of the colonial empires of Spain, France and England. While Spanish interest in the area lay dormant for close to two hundred years, France and Spain continued to trade control over this area during this period of time. This gave credence to the saying by the people in Louisiana that they were continually "tossed like a coin between Spain and France." Spain was willing to accept the last toss in an effort to defend its colonial empire in the Caribbean and areas bordering the Gulf of Mexico. The ever-present need for control of the Mississippi River was essential for protection from the encroaching Protestant English and American settlers.

The last period of Spanish control, from 1769 to 1803, witnessed a commingling of the Spanish and French Creoles, as the Europeans born in the New World were distinguished. Gradually, as Grace King related in her *A History of Louisiana*, "national and political differences became not only obliterated, but amalgamated in a common Creolism." However, it was the French language and culture that reigned supreme over the Spanish. This was the period when practices such as adhering to civil law rather than common law and naming political demarcations parishes rather than counties became firmly entrenched. This remains so even today.

With this variegated background in mind, the unique character of Baton Rouge monuments and the fierce loyalty of its citizens to them become easier to understand. However, it remains necessary to point out that Baton Rouge is the site of the only surviving Pentagon Barracks outside Washington, D.C., and that it proudly displays its participation in the wars fought by the United States. It also pays tribute to the state's sugar industry. Last but not least, it acknowledges its famous, or infamous, politicians who are recognized nationally and internationally. Baton Rouge also has the distinction of being the only state capital in the nation that has two of the most celebrated state capitol buildings. The first is the Old State Capitol, commissioned in 1847 and completed in 1850 at a cost of $400,000. The second is the New State Capitol, commissioned in January 1931 and completed in March 1932 at a cost of $5 million.

As a thoughtful aside, I pose a question: Have we gotten so involved in world affairs and present-day technology that we fail to read about the past and give it the recognition and merit that it so rightly deserves? This collection of significant and historical monuments that memorialize events and personages from the past and those of more recent times has experienced a lack of interest presently because of Baton Rouge's rapid and phenomenal growth in the last few decades. Despite their historical value and interest, these monuments and markers are largely unknown to contemporary Baton Rouge. In some small way, I hope this tome sparks some interest.

SUMMARY TABLE OF RELEVANT DATES AND CROSS REFERENCES FOR BATON ROUGE LANDMARKS AND MONUMENTS

Name of Landmark/ Monument	Date of Landmark/ Monument Dedication or Construction	Other Relevant Date(s) and Description	Cross Reference to Other Landmarks/ Monuments
Part I. Hidden Treasures			
Étienne de Boré's Sugar Kettle	1972	In 1794, heavy iron kettles were forged. In 1795, sugar was successfully granulated for the first time in kettles in Louisiana.	
Brass Figurehead from the Battleship USS *Louisiana*	1939	In 1902, the USS *Louisiana* was launched.	
Fort Sumter Saloon's Third Street Cannon	1861	In 1969, the cannon was excavated and it was discovered that it was a British pre–Revolutionary War one-thousand-pound carronade.	Civil War Brass Cannons (saw action at Fort Sumter)
Zachary Taylor's Homesite	1951	In 1848, Zachary Taylor was elected the twelfth president of the United States while living in Baton Rouge.	

Part II. Monuments of Famous Individuals			
Hebe	1914	In 1956, the Metro Council approved plans to beautify the grounds surrounding the statue of Hebe.	
Governor Henry Watkins Allen	1872	In 1864, Allen was elected governor of Louisiana only to serve a one-year term before the collapse of the Confederacy.	Old Louisiana State Capitol Building
Governor Huey Pierce Long	1940	In 1935, Long was assassinated at the New State Capitol Building.	New Louisiana State Capitol Building
Oliver Pollock	1979	In 1776, Pollock became an American citizen after the colonists declared independence from England. He became financier of the American Revolution.	Gálvez Plaza

Part III. Famous Historical Monuments			
Old Louisiana State Capitol Building	1849	In 1849, the building was completed. In 1855, the fence was completed. In 1973, it was designated a National Historic Landmark.	Henry Watkins Allen
Merci Train or French Gratitude Train or Friendship Train	1949	In 1947, the United States sent seven hundred boxcars of supplies (Friendship Trains) to France. In 1949, France responded to this kindness by sending forty-eight *Merci* Trains to the United States.	Old Louisiana State Capitol Building
New Louisiana State Capitol Building	1932	In 1931, the construction was initiated on the New State Capitol Building.	Governor Huey Pierce Long; Liberty Bell
Liberty Bell	1972	In 1950, the bell arrived in New Orleans. It was transferred to Baton Rouge in 1972.	New Louisiana State Capitol Building; Tower Clocks (refer to Appendix IV)
Gálvez Plaza	1979	In 1779, Gálvez captured British Fort Richmond and renamed it Fort San Carlos.	Oliver Pollock

Part IV. Famous Military Monuments			
Old Arsenal	1835	In 1886, the property was transferred to Louisiana State University.	Pentagon Barracks
Pentagon Barracks	1822	In 1819, the U.S. government purchased the land to begin a military post in Baton Rouge. It was completed in 1822.	Zachary Taylor's Homesite
Curtiss P-40 Warhawk, "Joy"	1987	In 1941, the plane saw its first combat.	USS *Kidd*
Memorial Tower, or Campanile, at Louisiana State University	1926	In 1923, the tower was built.	Tower Clocks (refer to Appendix IV); Hernando de Soto Statue (refer to Appendix V)
USS *Kidd* (DD-661)	1982	In 1943, the USS *Kidd* was commissioned and launched in New Jersey. In 1982, it arrived in Baton Rouge.	Curtiss P-40 Warhawk, "Joy"
Civil War Brass Cannons at LSU's Aerospace Studies and Military Science Building	1886	In 1886, William Tecumseh Sherman procured the two brass cannons and had them delivered to Louisiana State University.	Fort Sumter Saloon's Third Street Cannon

Part I

HIDDEN TREASURES

JEAN ÉTIENNE DE BORÉ'S SUGAR KETTLE

For close to two hundred years, sugar cane has been vital to Louisiana's economy. In fact, at one time this crop saved the struggling territory from financial disaster. It became so important to the livelihood of the area that the routine practices of its cultivation and harvest became inextricably woven into cultural and folkloric rituals. One of the best examples of this is the annual Sugar Cane Festival in New Iberia, which is on Bayou Teche and known as the Sugar Bowl of Louisiana. The festivities surrounding the planting and harvesting of the sugar cane gradually evolved into a formal festival in 1937, and now thirteen of the seventeen sugar-producing parishes participate in it. The festival always takes place on a weekend in September, usually starting with the blessing of the crop and a boat parade on Bayou Teche. This is followed by a children's parade the next afternoon, with the crowning of Queen Sugar at a ball on Saturday night, ending with a *fais-do-do*, or dance party. On Sunday, King Sucre and Queen Sugar reign over the final parade in New Iberia.

The very iron kettle that played a significant role in the development of this staple is at rest today, upside down, on a circular brick base in front of the Chemical Engineering Building on the campus of Louisiana State University (LSU) in Baton Rouge. If it were not for the historical marker that identifies it, most of the students hurrying past might regard it as just another discarded black iron pot.

This particular kettle, however, is anything but ordinary. Its picture has appeared in countless magazines, including *National Geographic*, as a symbolic

De Boré's sugar kettle as it is today. *Photo by Zozaya.*

memorial to the birth of the sugar industry in Louisiana. For this is the kettle that Monsieur Jean Étienne de Boré used in 1795 to successfully granulate sugar here for the first time. What transpired that December day within the kettle's rim was the culmination of the efforts of about fifty years of repeated attempts to crystallize the syrupy, mud-colored liquid that oozed from the sugar cane. It should also pay tribute to the man who refused to yield to the agony of defeat.

When this triumphant experiment occurred, the huge kettle was located on De Boré's plantation near New Orleans, close to the present site of Audubon Park. The state of Louisiana was in virtual economic ruin. Its staple crop, indigo, had been left naked and desolate as caterpillars ate their way through all of the planted fields. De Boré's estate was no exception, for he lost the small fortune he had invested in the plants that yielded the blue dye.

One of those rare men destined to alter the course of events, Étienne de Boré refused to be daunted by this failure. Although a member of the old Norman nobility and educated in France, he seems to have been imbued with the pioneering spirit of his birthplace in Kaskaskia, Illinois. In addition, his ten years of service as a *mousquetaire* in the household troops of the king of France had given his personal discipline a military bent.

Maybe it was a combination of these qualities and his belief in his personal destiny that made De Boré persist in his dream of raising sugar cane in Louisiana. The agricultural quarterlies of that time discouraged this dream, expressing the opinion that Louisiana's climate was too severe. One of the quarterlies even stated, "It is an incontestable fact and important truth that the soil of Lower Louisiana is not adaptable to raise cane, and fine sugar will never be made here." Despite this and the dire forebodings of his wife and friends, the fifty-year-old De Boré forged ahead with his plan. He purchased seed cane from two Spanish friends in Santo Domingo, Señor Mendez and Señor Solis, and proceeded in 1794 with the cultivation of the "tall, sweet grass." As if to further demonstrate that he was ignoring the past attempts that had failed to granulate sugar, he gave the order to forge the heavy iron kettles in which to boil the juice crushed from the sugar cane.

So much was at stake that those interested and curious gathered one year later on that blustery winter day when the Frenchman decided to finalize his experiment. The cane juice was poured into the very kettle that is housed off South Stadium Drive in Baton Rouge today. The fire under it roared as the partially clad slaves took turns stirring the liquid while clouds of steam enveloped them. During this test, which some say De Boré learned how to do from his friends Mendez and Solis, the brownish "marmalade" began changing in texture. With the crowd of elegantly dressed onlookers anxiously waiting, De Boré grabbed the paddle, held it higher and shouted dramatically, "It granulates! It granulates! See for yourselves!"

In the excitement that followed, as everyone rushed to taste and feel the sugar, the paddle was set on the rim of the kettle, and both of them were temporarily forgotten. By the end of the year, however, this victorious experiment had brought Monsieur de Boré $12,000. It also influenced and encouraged other planters to follow his example, and sugar cane quickly supplanted all other crops in Louisiana. Soon, as Governor William C. Claiborne wrote to Thomas Jefferson, the sugar planters were amassing wealth with a facility that was "almost incredible." Sugar cane had become king in Louisiana.

Étienne de Boré continued to use his rescued sugar kettle for further experiments until his death in 1820. By this time, his plantation had become the hub for the rapidly expanding sugar cane industry. During the Civil War, unfortunately, the De Boré estate was decimated. Rumor has it that the kettle succumbed then to the dubious honor of being used by Ulysses S. Grant's brother-in-law to make tafia, a form of white lightning, for his soldiers. When the Union army left, the black pot was left to sink in the plantation mud.

De Boré's sugar kettle, discovered by John Hill. *Courtesy of the State Library of Louisiana Historic Photograph Collection.*

The crudely crafted kettle was saved from this ignominious end years later when it was unearthed and purchased by John Hill, a West Baton Rouge planter, as junk for his iron foundry. Miraculously, he saw the faded inscription identifying it as the sugar vat that De Boré had used in his successful experiment to granulate sugar. Instead of melting the kettle as had been intended, Mr. Hill proceeded to donate it to the state. Officials had it placed on the grounds of the Old State Capitol in Baton Rouge, where it was "thrown around hither and yon as junk." When Thomas Boyd, then president of Louisiana State University, heard about this mistreatment, he rescued the old kettle and set it proudly on the front lawn of his residence on the old university campus, former site of the Old Pentagon Barracks.

Louisiana State University moved to its new campus in 1926, and so did the sugar kettle. The students first rolled it out to the Agriculture Hall. Later, it was mounted near Alumni Hall. The mammoth open kettle was moved once again in 1972, this time to its present location close to the Chemical Engineering Building and the Audubon "Sugar"

Factory. This should be its final sojourn since it certainly seems to be its most appropriate resting place. Both the sugar kettle and the Chemical Engineering Department, an outgrowth of the Audubon Sugar School that had evolved from a state experimental station and factory, had their origins on the same De Boré plantation.

Furthermore, it is most befitting that the kettle should be ensconced here to highlight Louisiana State University's pioneering work in sugar engineering. Led by Dr. Charles E. Coates, LSU established the first chemical engineering courses offered by any university in the United States. This was only the genesis of the continuous role that this university was to play in the development of the sugar cane industry to its present high level of productivity—an invaluable boost to Louisiana's agrarian economy. It's no wonder that at the 1972 ceremony dedicating the sugar kettle, it was acclaimed as paying a "proud yet unceremonious tribute to the start of something big."

An important footnote to history should be added here. Étienne de Boré was the first person to hold the title of mayor of New Orleans. He was appointed mayor by Governor William C. Claiborne in 1803. He only served one year, resigning in 1804 to take care of his personal affairs. However, he continued to enrich the fabric of Louisiana's life through his progeny. His grandson, Charles Étienne Arthur Gayarré, was born in 1805 at the De Boré plantation, known today as Audubon Park, a suburb of New Orleans. Charles Étienne Arthur Gayarré studied law in Pennsylvania and was admitted to the bar. He was elected to the Louisiana House of Representatives, appointed the Louisiana deputy attorney general and became presiding judge of the New Orleans City Court. While Gayarré was elected to the Senate of the United States in 1834, ill health forced him to resign without ever taking his seat. His political contributions notwithstanding, it was Charles Gayarré's historical writings that brought him enduring fame as the acknowledged "historian" of Louisiana. His four-volume *A History of Louisiana*, a republication and expansion of his previous works in the historical field, is a comprehensive history of Louisiana from the time of its discovery to 1861.

BRASS FIGUREHEAD FROM THE
BATTLESHIP USS *LOUISIANA*

When Theodore Roosevelt was president of the United States at the dawn of the twentieth century, he was responsible for launching a large battle fleet in the Pacific Ocean. Ostensibly, this was a global peacetime cruise to show the world that while he might speak softly, he could and would "carry a big stick." This battle fleet consisted of sixteen white battleships, plus their auxiliary craft, and was intended and designed to reflect the power and might of the United States Navy. It correspondingly became known as the Great White Fleet. Louisiana's segment of this piece of Americana rests today in an unusual monument marking the entrance to City Park at Dalrymple Drive and Park Boulevard in Baton Rouge.

Dedicated to the veterans of the Spanish-American War, the looming concrete memorial was fashioned to resemble the prow of the United States battleship *Louisiana*, once an integral part of the stalwart naval force that toured this hemisphere in 1907. A massive, solid brass figurehead that once embellished the actual prow of this proud battleship dominates this monument. The five- by eight-foot insignia, a replica of the Great Seal of the United States, shares the concrete base with three other plaques.

Brass figurehead on the bow of the USS *Louisiana. Photo by Layne Photography.*

One of the plaques is cast from the metal recovered from the USS *Maine* and notes, "In Memoriam, USS Maine destroyed in Havana Harbor, Feb. 15, 1898." In the center of the second plaque are inscribed the following words: "Spanish American War veterans, 1898–1902." It is the third and most prominent marker that gives an inkling of the series of mishaps that have pursued this discarded ornamental brass work. Boldly, though erroneously, it asserts that the monument was erected in 1539, predating the founding of Baton Rouge by more than 150 years. What should have been a C in Roman numerals, recording 1939 as the correct date, was cast as a D. We can only surmise what consternation occurred when it was discovered that the plaque registered a 400-year-old monument in a city that was only about 250 years old.

The USS *Louisiana* was launched in 1902 in Newport News, Rhode Island. Only eight years later, in 1910, Theodore Roosevelt's ostentatious task fleet succumbed to the demands for camouflage. The white paint on all U.S. Navy ships was replaced by "battleship gray." Simultaneously, orders were also issued to remove all distinguishing and ornamental brass work from the ships. It was then that the USS *Louisiana* was stripped of its figurehead and the accompanying brass designs that extended thirty feet on either side of its prow. Logically, the relics of this battleship were crated and shipped to the capital city of the state for which it had been named.

In the beginning, the heavy brass work ended up at the Old State Capitol Building. At first, the figurehead was placed on the west side of the capitol grounds, positioned in such a manner that it overlooked the Mississippi River. The rest of the ornamental scrollwork, according to some old accounts, was situated by convict labor in a rock garden and grotto that surrounded the figurehead. There it all remained, virtually unnoticed, until the Old State Capitol grounds were renovated, possibly in 1937 by the Works Progress Administration. Then both the figurehead and scrollwork were removed and ignominiously stored in the capitol basement, replaced by a terrace of rosebushes.

By this time, the battleship proudly bearing our state's name had been declared obsolete. In 1922, in keeping with the nation's disarmament policy following the First World War, it was scrapped. All that remained of the USS *Louisiana* lay gathering dust and mildew in the basement of our old state capitol. Since for a while it appeared that no one wanted the abandoned emblem either, it seemed destined for the scrapheap. Fortunately for Baton Rouge historians, J. St. Clair Favrot, Louisiana's adjutant and service commissioner for the Spanish-American War veterans, learned of the plight of the brass medallion and plaques. He was appalled that this historic figurehead, which weighed several tons and had originally cost the United States government $17,000 in 1907, had been relegated to this state of neglect and oblivion. He vowed to correct this situation.

Justifiably, Mr. Favrot thought that the figurehead should be used in a permanent memorial to the men from this area who fought in the Spanish-American War. To accomplish this end, he won the support of the Lee-Scott Camp No. 6, United Spanish-American War veterans. The entrance to

City Park, which was a hub for social activities then, was selected as the site befitting the concrete testimonial. Frederick von Osthoff, Louisiana State University's assistant dean of administration, designed the structure, while the city engineer, L.H. Voorhies, supervised its construction. A Lee-Scott Camp member, August Ledoux, performed most of the volunteer labor. The monument was finished just in time for its unveiling on May 17, 1939.

The white prow-shaped monument attracts attention now mainly because of its curious shape. Few Baton Rouge citizens are aware that part of it once sailed the seven seas as a piece of a mighty and intimidating American naval fleet. Even fewer know that Secretary of War Harry Woodring was invited to preside at its formal dedication in 1939, attesting to the importance given the memorial at the time. Presently, although the concrete base is cracked in places and the weighty brass is tarnished by time and weather, the figurehead monument remains one of Baton Rouge's most unique landmarks.

FORT SUMTER SALOON'S THIRD STREET CANNON

Fort Sumter Saloon's Third Street Cannon, next to a fire hydrant. *Photo by Layne Photography.*

As if in keeping with a master plan, and despite all odds, some things seem destined to survive the devastation of the passage of time and associated change. Such is the case of the cannon that is partially embedded in the pavement close to the intersection of Riverside Mall and Laurel Street. Some claim that it is a pre–Revolutionary War carronade, while others assert that it is a piece of Spanish artillery captured in 1810 when the Baton Rouge fort was taken by General Philemon Thomas. Currently almost hidden from view by a fire hydrant, the cannon is distinguished by an official Baton Rouge Historic Marker:

Hidden Treasures

According to local tradition,
Charles Wieck named his
newly purchased saloon
the day after Fort Sumter
was fired on, 1861
and put the cannon
out front for atmosphere.
It was one of the city's
most popular saloons
until prohibition.

This simple statement glosses over the cannon's early years in downtown Baton Rouge. Mr. Wieck opened his saloon on the very day that the Confederate army under Louisiana's own General P.G.T. Beauregard opened fire on Fort Sumter in Charleston Harbor on April 1861, initiating the Civil War. Following that time, it stood as a silent sentinel to the activity and merriment that surrounded it. There is no clue to how it managed to survive and remain in place through the various pavings and sidewalk changes that occurred in the growing city. There isn't even a slight hint of why there was such a hue and cry raised by enraged citizens when the old war piece was removed by the Department of Public Works on a winter day in 1969.

What was there about the old muzzleloader that evoked such fierce devotion in the Baton Rouge community? Charles Wieck, who offhandedly had placed the obsolete cannon in front of his saloon as a colorful attraction, would probably have chuckled with amazement that its removal 108 years later

Fort Sumter Saloon's Third Street Cannon. *Photo by Layne Photography.*

would erupt in a major controversy. In fact, the controversy grew to such proportions that before it was resolved and the cannon returned to its original resting place, Mayor Woodrow "Woody" Dumas, Parish Attorney Gordon Kean and Department of Public Works Director Ray Burgess were all forced to become involved.

But let us return to that balmy day in April when Mr. Wieck purchased the old Rainbow House Saloon. Fort Sumter had just been fired upon, and he wanted to memorialize this event. First, he renamed his saloon after the fort that had been attacked. Then, he went to the local garrison commander and asked for the extinct firearm, which was gladly given to him. Placing the cannon in front of his newly christened Fort Sumter Saloon, Wieck thus gave his establishment "a more military flavor in keeping with its name." He proceeded to make his saloon the finest in Baton Rouge and succeeded until prohibition closed its doors in 1920.

During prohibition, the Fort Sumter Saloon was converted into an office building and became known as the Wieck Building. Still, the cannon remained in its original place in front of this building. Subsequent changes deigned to leave the archaic weapon untouched. City fathers were said to have left the cannon at its spot in order to keep vehicles off one of the few good sidewalks existing in the city at the time.

On a fateful day, January 15, 1969, as part of the reconstruction of the busy downtown intersection, the Department of Public Works excavated the old cannon. Department Director Ray Burgess immediately regretted this act, for he had to spend the entire next day "calming the wrath" of persons who demanded that the cannon be put right back. Baton Rouge Mayor Woody Dumas was also besieged with indignant callers. Not only were civic groups contacting him berating the cannon's removal, but private concerns were also beleaguering him with offers to purchase it. The mayor responded by referring the matter to the Baton Rouge City/Parish Council and asking Parish Attorney Gordon Kean for a ruling on who had the jurisdiction to decide the cannon's fate. In the meantime, Director Burgess played it safe and locked the antique muzzleloader at the city's Valley Park Warehouse.

The City Beautification Commission and the Foundation for Historical Louisiana became "hysterical." Gone was their dream, they feared, of placing a historical marker by the cannon. Everyone now listened to varying proposals concerning what to do with the cannon. The proposals germinated like wildfire, for there was unbelievable interest now in the landmark that previously had been overlooked by most. Mayor Dumas suggested that the venerable cannon be given to the Louisiana Arts and Science Museum—much to the delight of its director, Adelaide Brent. One civic organization wanted the cannon placed and mounted on the Old State Capitol grounds, while another group endorsed the plan to display it at Port Hudson.

The proposals for displaying the antique cannon were in keeping with the findings of the Pelican Arms Society. According to one of the officials of the local gun club, it seemed "a pity to bury such a relic in the ground, especially one as intact and in good condition as this one." These antique arms collectors conducted a study on the cannon and discovered that it was believed to be a British pre–Revolutionary War one-thousand-pound naval carronade.

In the meantime, the daily newspaper conducted a poll to help determine what the citizens of Baton Rouge wanted done with the carronade. Letters poured in voicing opinions, one from as far away as Pago Pago in the South Pacific. They voted to return the landmark to its original location.

The "war" over the obsolete cannon came to an end when the city council voted to half-bury the cannon again as close as possible to the original location where Wieck had embedded it. One month and eleven days after it had been dug up, Director Burgess presided over its reinterment. Judging from the smile on his face, an observer noted that Burgess "no doubt prayed that he too would be part of Baton Rouge history before it is moved again." And so the puzzle over the sudden devotion to the cannon was also resolved. It seems that civic-minded citizens in Baton Rouge simply did not want to part with this interesting part of their history.

ZACHARY TAYLOR'S HOMESITE

High on a bluff overlooking the Mississippi River across from the New State Capitol in Baton Rouge stands a simple marker:

To Honor
ZACHARY TAYLOR
U.S. Army General and Twelfth President
Of the United States
Known to Americans as
"OLD ROUGH AND READY"
And who lived for a time some 255 yards

Southwest of this spot
This Marker placed in 1951 by
Camps of Louisiana
WOODMEN OF THE WORLD

While living here, in 1848, he was elected twelfth president of the United States.

A Virginian by birth and reared in Kentucky, this renowned soldier and future president of the United States adopted Louisiana as his state and referred to Baton Rouge as his "hometown." The marker commemorates the spot where the modest three-room cottage, with its surrounding veranda and domestic outbuildings, once stood proudly as the official residence of the Zachary Taylor family.

Zachary Taylor homesite marker. *Photo by Layne Photography.*

28

Zachary Taylor's close association with Louisiana began in 1809, when he served as first lieutenant in the Seventh Infantry of the U.S. Army. As a soldier, he was slated to be stationed and transferred in and out of Louisiana many times. In the process, he formed an attachment for this area that he held for no other. His bond with the city was firmly cemented in 1822 when he took command of the First Infantry garrison. While serving at this post, the young Taylor supervised the construction of new barracks. These quarters, known today as the Pentagon Barracks, have become a historic landmark in Baton Rouge.

The native Virginian become so attached to this area that he soon purchased 380 acres of land in West Feliciana and added to this acreage whenever possible. The energetic and enterprising soldier became a planter in this area also. Consequently, regardless of where he was stationed in his military career, he used his furloughs to inspect his plantations along the Mississippi River bottomlands.

Zachary Taylor returned to Baton Rouge in November 1840 when he was granted a transfer from his post in Florida. He declined the use of the most ostentatious quarters offered him at the Pentagon Barracks. Instead, he set up residence with his wife and six children at the nearby frame bungalow whose location we acknowledge and note today. At the time the Taylor family moved in, the house was known as the "Spanish cottage" because it had been originally inhabited by a proud captain from Castile.

The Taylor family joined in the activities of the small local community. As a result, Lieutenant Colonel Zachary Taylor formed a close friendship with John Baptist Kleinpeter, a prominent Baton Rouge banker of the era and owner of the Hard Times plantation located on present-day Highland Road. This friendship proved to be so meaningful that the two men exchanged portraits. Copies of these portraits are included in the 1975 edition of *Louisiana Portraits Bicentennial Edition.*

The pioneer soldier was now military commander of the Southwestern Department, an area that included the present-day states of Oklahoma, Arkansas and Louisiana, as well as southern Missouri. The location of his post dictated his immediate involvement in the Mexican-American War in 1846. Taylor's military genius helped him win the Battles of Palo Alto and Resaca de la Palma and capture the Mexican cities of Matamoras and Monterrey. These victories gained him spontaneous national acclaim and the rank of major general.

Despite his greatly reduced forces, Taylor defeated vastly superior Mexican forces at Buena Vista. "Old Rough and Ready," as his soldiers had nicknamed him, captured the national imagination, and his fame spread like wildfire. The veteran soldier who had no previous political experience became a promising candidate for the presidency of the United States. On a wave of popular enthusiasm produced by his military victories, a somewhat bewildered Zachary Taylor was elected to the highest office in 1849.

General Taylor's triumphant return to Baton Rouge from the Mexican-American War marked his final military assignment. Fortunately, the famous lithographer Louis J.M. Daguerre recorded the celebrated general's last days here. His lithograph presents a faithful picture of the old soldier standing in front of the galleried house under a tree, gazing at two of his war horses grazing contentedly. This serene picture, however, doesn't reflect the wild anticipation and excitement that surrounded Taylor during the presidential race. Even the steamships cruising along the Mississippi River would stop in front of his humble-looking abode hoping to catch a glimpse of its famous occupant.

It was during these occasions, according to some old accounts, that Taylor's favorite horse, Old Whitney, pranced gracefully along the bluff. With the breeze rippling his mane, it appeared that he was acknowledging the honors paid to his master.

On a bleak January morning in 1849, after he was elected president of the United States, Zachary Taylor took his formal leave of Baton Rouge, saying:

> *Gentlemen, I assure you it is with feelings of no ordinary character that I meet with my fellow citizens on this occasion, many of whom I have known for more than a quarter of a century. Had I consulted my own wishes, I should have much preferred to retain the office I am now about to vacate, and have remained among you.*

Unfortunately, President Taylor was not destined to return to Baton Rouge, for he died unexpectedly within a year after his election. His untimely death was quite a loss to our city, state and nation. It left a vacuum in the many areas he had served faithfully and courageously for forty years.

GOVERNOR HENRY WATKINS ALLEN

The "pink" shaft of marble that rises from the north section of the Old State Capitol grounds about twenty-five feet from the highest terrace and the surrounding fence is the only monument on these grounds besides the Capitol Building itself. It is the tomb of Henry Watkins Allen, who unquestionably was one of Louisiana's most respected and beloved governors. He was born in Virginia, educated in Missouri and practiced law in Mississippi. Somehow, he got involved and fought in the Texas Revolution against Mexico. He returned up north to Cambridge, studied law at Harvard and then returned to Texas, where he was elected to the Texas House of Representatives in 1846. Later, he decided to move to Louisiana.

Immediately, he began to share the expertise that he had acquired during his studies and travels and endeared himself to Louisianans. While he was traveling in Europe in 1853 and collecting information for his *Travels of a Sugar Planter*, he was elected to the Louisiana legislature during his absence from the state. Upon his return to Louisiana, he became actively engaged in the

Governor H.W. Allen Memorial.
Photo by Layne Photography.

proceedings of that governmental body. One of his projects during this time was to embellish the Old State Capitol and its grounds, the latter with plants that he had discovered and brought back from his travels. Unfortunately, because of the outbreak of the Civil War in 1861, Allen never had the opportunity to serve in this building after he was elected governor in 1864.

When Louisiana seceded from the Union in 1861, Allen joined the Confederate army as a lieutenant colonel on August 15 of that year. By March 1, 1862, he had been promoted to colonel and, by August 1863, to brigadier general. Early on, he garnered a reputation as an exceptional military leader who fought alongside his troops until his critical war injuries prevented him from continuing in this role. During the Battle of Baton Rouge, both of his legs were severely wounded, and he later lost one of them. The injuries occurred on August 5, 1862, on the corner of Government Street and South Nineteenth Street while he was leading his Louisiana brigade against an Indiana battery. Sarah Morgan wrote in her Civil War diary after she met Colonel Allen in November 1862 that he was a "wee little man" with a "pasty face." Despite these physical attributes, just three years after Louisiana seceded from the Union, he was elected governor of the Confederate portion of the state. He would only serve one year, losing his office when the Confederacy collapsed in 1865.

During his term of office, Governor Allen worked incessantly and tirelessly to improve conditions in the state. He attempted to develop manufacturing in the state by building a framework for state stores, factories and foundries that were to be kept in operation by civilians after the war. He was able to get the legislature to enact a law prohibiting illegal impressments of citizens by Confederate agents. Both with private donations and public funds, he established hospitals and provided disabled soldiers with a stipend of eleven dollars monthly. Since medicines were so scarce during the Civil War, he commissioned Dr. Bartholomew Egan to begin a laboratory that would produce medicine for the army. Dr. Egan was able to buy out the facilities of Mount Lebanon Female College in Bienville Parish and immediately started producing turpentine, castor oil, opium, carbonate of soda and medicinal grades of whiskey. (This facility was closed after the Civil War ended.) In addition, Allen supervised a covert operation to procure vital medical supplies, such as quinine, from behind Union lines in New Orleans.

At the end of the Civil War, the Louisiana governor initiated conciliatory actions to aid in the healing process following the armed conflict. For example, arrangements were made with General Edmund Kirby-Smith to transfer all the cotton and sugar that had been collected by Confederate agents during the war into the state coffers. This was to be a tax-in-kind until the Louisiana Confederate debt to the Union could be paid. Before leaving office, Governor Allen wanted to help the state become self-sufficient, with civil liberties intact. According to historian John Winters, when Allen was declared an outlaw by the Union military forces and thus subject to death if captured, he was forced to leave the state as soon as possible. Before doing so, he took the time to address the citizens of Louisiana and begged them to submit to the inevitable and start life anew.

The now bankrupt former Governor Allen opted to go to Mexico in a self-imposed exile. While in Mexico City, his business acumen led him to assist in opening up trade between Mexico and Texas. He also successfully started an English-language newspaper. But time, military injuries and ill health finally prevailed, and Louisiana's former governor died in Mexico in 1866, a few days short of his forty-sixth birthday. Initially, he was buried in Mexico. His friends here in Louisiana, who had always maintained contact with him, would not rest until they brought his body back to Louisiana. He was buried quietly in New Orleans in 1867, denied the fanfare he so richly deserved by the Federal forces. While in New Orleans, his body was disinterred and interred four different times before a proper monument could be erected. By 1870, the Allen Monumental Association had been formed for the express purpose of erecting a proper monument over Henry Watkins Allen's grave. This was accomplished by 1872. Constructed of Missouri granite, the monument itself weighed five and a half tons. His epitaph and inscriptions had already been chiseled into the stone.

The city of Baton Rouge still grieved over the loss of its beloved general and former governor. After Reconstruction, a group of citizens started a movement to bring Allen's remains to Baton Rouge and bury him on the grounds of the newly rebuilt Old State Capitol. This act would show the world the high esteem in which Allen was held. In 1884, the Louisiana legislature appropriated $1,000 to effect this change. When the casket and the monument arrived in Baton Rouge on a June day in 1885, the five-foot-high brick foundation and tomb, with an opening on the west side for the casket, were ready to receive Governor Allen's remains. After reinterment, the monument rose to thirty feet above the ground, without Allen's bust, as had been intended, but with a tall, shapely finial instead.

The pomp and military circumstance with which Governor Allen was finally laid to rest in full Confederate uniform attest to the respect, affection and adulation that the citizens of Louisiana still wanted to show him, even four years after his death. His epitaph, submitted by one of his friends, reads as follows:

*Your friends are proud to know that Louisiana had a Governor
who with an opportunity of securing a million dollars in gold
preferred being honest in a foreign land without one cent.*

The honors accorded to Henry Watkins Allen have continued over the years, as evidenced by the number of plaques and memorials named for him throughout the state of Louisiana. The one closest to Baton Rouge, and just across the Mississippi River, is at the city of Port Allen, which was named after him.

GOVERNOR HUEY PIERCE LONG

To build a monument to a Louisiana governor who was simultaneously venerated and intensely detested presented a special set of challenges. Huey Pierce Long, who was governor of the state from 1928 until 1932 and later Louisiana's senator from 1932 until his assassination in 1935, aroused the heights and depths of human emotion as no other politician in Louisiana had done. To the poor and downtrodden whom he championed, he was a saint. To everyone else, those he betrayed and nullified, he was the devil incarnate. It was extremely difficult to reconcile the intensity of the diverse emotions. However, there was no denying that this son of Louisiana had put the state of Louisiana "on the map" of the United States, so to speak.

Huey Long captured national attention and imagination when he incorporated the Share Our Wealth Society and copyrighted the slogan "Every Man a King." His programs of reform challenged the existing Louisiana political hierarchy, which consisted of Louisiana upper-income groups, Standard Oil, gas and shipping interests all allied with the New Orleans Old Regulars. Instead, he projected and propelled the social programs of Franklin Delano Roosevelt's New Deal.

Louisiana in the middle of the 1920s was in the throes of the Great Depression and could hardly be called a modern state. It was ready for a leader who would demand change. The programs its new governor promised would do just that. Dating from the time he was elected in 1928 until his death in 1935, Louisiana had greatly increased its appropriations for higher education. Enrollment in public schools had increased by 20 percent, a direct result of state provision of free textbooks and free lunches. For the first time, Louisiana had adequate roads and bridges. State hospitals were enlarged and their facilities increased. The poll tax was repealed, allowing for a broader base of new voters. The poor people of the state could ill afford to be concerned that these improvements had been made by riding roughshod over political principles and individuals. They were not concerned, either, with the fact that the Long program, anticipating the New Deal, was implemented by incurring tremendous expenditures. These had to be met by heavier taxes, particularly on corporations, and the issuance of state bonds rose to an astronomical figure. Despite all of this, Huey Long's party platform soon combined with his magnetic, forceful, explosive personality to pose a threat to the presidency of Franklin Delano Roosevelt.

Governor Long's intense desire to improve the quality of life in Louisiana and promote its national recognition necessarily involved his association with the state university. Louisiana State University Agricultural & Mechanical College had originated with several land grants made by the government of the United States in 1806, 1811 and 1827, to establish a seminary of learning. In 1853, the Louisiana General Assembly created the Seminary of Learning of the State of Louisiana near Pineville, Louisiana. It was opened January 2, 1860, with General William Tecumseh Sherman as its superintendent. When Louisiana became the sixth state to secede from the Union, Sherman had to resign his position, and the school was forced to close in 1861.

For all intents and purposes, the Seminary of Learning of the State of Louisiana remained closed until 1865, when it was reopened in Pineville. When the Pineville campus building burned down in 1869, the institution was moved to Baton Rouge and was housed at the Institute for the Deaf, Dumb and Blind. In 1870, the seminary changed its official title to the Louisiana State University. In 1874, a legislative act established Louisiana State University Agricultural & Mechanical College to carry out the 1862 provisions of the United States Morrill Act granting lands for educational purposes. The college was opened temporarily at the University of Louisiana in New Orleans in 1874. In 1876, legislative acts #103 and #145 combined the University of Louisiana and Louisiana Agricultural College until they were merged with Louisiana State University in 1877. This prompted the final name change to Louisiana State University Agricultural & Mechanical College (LSU). LSU then became a land-grant institution, and the title of superintendent was changed to president.

When Huey Pierce Long was elected governor in 1928, LSU was a small country school, labeled a "third rate" institution by the Association of State Universities. It had only 1,800 students and 168 faculty members, with an annual operating budget of $800,000. By 1930, Governor Long had become painfully aware of this situation and responded by initiating a massive building program on the campus. He expanded the physical plant and added educational departments. By 1937, Louisiana State University was ranked eleventh among state universities and twentieth in the nation in size. It had 7,000 students, and the size of the faculty had tripled to include 400 professors. The band, with only 28 members in 1928, grew to be 250 strong, the largest state university marching band in the nation, with the most expensive uniforms money could buy. Huey replaced the band director with his friend, Castro Carazo, who had been the Roosevelt Hotel's orchestra leader. Together, they composed two musical works, "Touchdown for LSU" and "Darling of LSU." Huey financed most of these improvements by negotiating with the State of Louisiana to purchase acreage from the old LSU campus adjoining the New State Capitol Building in downtown Baton Rouge. To do so, he diverted $9.0 million from the state budget to spend the money on LSU's expansion, increasing its annual operating budget to $2.8 million.

The list could go on and on. Governor Long could be well satisfied that he had brought Louisiana to national attention by his aggressive acts of improvement. The manner in which he accomplished it remains a subject of debate. He figured out inventive ways to "rob Peter to pay Paul." Leaders of his pet projects were told to build or create what they needed to realize their dreams and that he would find the money necessary to fund them. He didn't seem to worry about what worthy causes he would deprive of funds in order to provide for these clandestine operations. Governor Long seemed to follow the suggestion of Niccolò di Bernado dei Machiavelli, the fifteenth-century Florentine writer, who espoused the theory that "the ends justify the means." Regardless, how could such a man be ignored or obliterated in death? Once again, mankind attempted to define itself and the respective struggles that the Great Depression was posing—hindering, among other things, efforts to build a great university—by paying homage to its former Governor Long and erecting a statue in his honor.

And so the task began. Since he had been shot on Sunday, September 8, 1935, in the corridor of the New State Capitol Building and died thirty-one hours later, there didn't seem to be any question but that his grave site should be on the grounds of the skyscraper that he had been largely instrumental in constructing. His funeral and burial took place there on September 12, 1935. At first, it was a very simple grave. Its only distinguishing feature was the light from a spotlight that illuminated it at night. The beam, originating midway up the capitol's tower, has been shining on the grave since shortly after Huey was buried.

By the spring of 1937, public sentiment was such that Governor Richard Leche, who had been elected governor on a Huey Long political platform, invited artists and sculptors to submit designs for a statue that would be the centerpiece for a memorial over Long's grave site. A Huey P. Long Memorial Commission was formed and began its task to complete a suitable memorial for its fallen leader, announcing that the entire cost for the project would be assumed by the late senator's friends. An American sculptor from New York, Charles Keck, was selected and commissioned for the job based on his national reputation for statues of Abraham Lincoln and "Stonewall" Jackson.

In 1938, notwithstanding the memorial commission's promise that the funds for the project would come from Senator Long's friends, the Louisiana legislature appropriated $50,000 to finance the endeavor. The thirty-five-foot memorial was erected and unveiled on March 21, 1940, nearly five years after Long's death. It stands directly in the center of the sunken garden across from the New State Capitol. The bronze figure seems to gaze across the manicured lawn and gardens toward the capitol, his hands appearing to reach for and touch the building.

Governor Huey P. Long. *Photo by Zozaya.*

Governor Huey P. Long. *Photo by Zozaya.*

The base of the statue is white granite. Portrayed in bas relief on the marble base are scenes from the political life of the governor and later senator. Inscribed in the front with Long's name is a rearing horse carrying a pennant bearing Long's popular motto "Share the Wealth." The sides of the base depict him with builders planning public works and with children extending the scope of public education. The rear of the base gives his dates of office, a short eulogy and words from an address he made to the United States Senate on March 8, 1935, giving some insight into the man:

> *I know the hearts of the people because I have not colored my own.*
> *I know when I am right in my own conscience.*
> *I have one language. Its simplicity gains pardon for my lack of letters.*
> *Fear will not change it. Persecution will not change it.*
> *It cannot be changed while people suffer.*

The marble base is surmounted by a twelve-foot bronze statue of Huey Pierce Long. His son, Senator Russell Long, posed for it. The impressive bronze stands on the marble base beside miniatures of the New State Capitol and the Mississippi River Bridge accompanied by models of graduates in caps and gowns.

OLIVER POLLOCK

The ten-foot-tall bronze facial sculpture of Oliver Pollock, set high on a pedestal, gazes intently over Gálvez Plaza in downtown Baton Rouge, as if surveying everything in sight. The deep, penetrating eyes seem to reflect the glories and despair of things won and lost. Who is this American Patriot so few of us know about and recognize?

Oliver Pollock was born in Ireland in 1737. He immigrated to the United States and settled in Pennsylvania in 1760. Bright and energetic and with an eye for business, he soon started trading with the Spanish West Indies and became fluent in Spanish. In 1768, he moved to New Orleans to further his merchant trade and quickly became a wealthy New Orleans merchant, with several plantations along the Mississippi River. There was an added benefit: from this New Orleans location, before Spain declared war on England, he could continue his secretive, undercover aid to the American colonists.

Facial sculpture of Oliver Pollock. *Photo by Layne Photography.*

Then, in 1776, when the American colonists declared their independence from England, Pollock quickly became an American citizen.

In 1769, Spain sent its best general to Louisiana to quell the insurrection of 1768 against the first Spanish governor, Don Antonio de Ulloa. When Spanish Captain General Alejandro O'Reilly arrived in New Orleans, he renewed his friendship with Oliver Pollock. Not only had the two men met before in Havana, but they had also discovered their mutual Irish ancestry and experienced the same anti-Catholic bigotry. So, when Spanish Captain General Alejandro O'Reilly became Governor O'Reilly and desperately needed flour to feed his troops, Pollock was happy to sell him the flour at cost. Pollock continued a similar relationship with the next Spanish governor, Luis de Unzaga. As purchasing agent for the Continental Congress in New Orleans and as New Orleans agent for the Commonwealth of Virginia, Pollock could secretly supply the colonists, aided by the Spanish, with provisions and dry goods—muskets, bayonets, gunpowder, blankets and medicinal drugs, especially quinine.

When Bernardo de Gálvez replaced Unzaga as the Spanish governor to Louisiana in 1777, Oliver Pollock was able to again continue the same easy, mutually beneficial relationship with him. Both men were driven by an identical desire to see their common enemy, Great Britain, fail. In 1779, news spread that England had declared war on Spain. The need for subterfuge was over, and Governor Gálvez had orders from Spain to protect New Orleans and the mouth of the Mississippi River at all costs. Pollock became his aide-de-camp in the now famous Marcha de Gálvez and the capture of the British Fort Richmond in Baton Rouge, renamed Fort San Carlos. One of Pollock's significant contributions at this point was to successfully request that his friends in British Natchez surrender to Gálvez's superior forces and spare further bloodshed. Therefore, when Baton Rouge capitulated, the terms of surrender included Fort Panmure at Natchez.

Oliver Pollock, also referred to as the western financier of the American Revolution, whose contributions ultimately exceeded $300,000, was now insolvent. Neither the Continental Congress nor the Commonwealth of Virginia had the funds to repay the expenditures that he had personally made to outfit ships, naval contingents, small Continental armies and the aforementioned supplies. Still, he refused a colonel's commission in the Spanish army and the handsome salary that accompanied it. Later, Pollock wrote, "I felt it my duty to decline this offer, the feeble services which, with nine brothers Americans, I had been able to render were under the banners of America. We took them with us into the field."

At this phase in his life, Pollock did accept a position as commercial agent for the United States in Havana, Cuba. While there, his creditors in New Orleans petitioned the governor of Havana to imprison him until he paid his debts to them. He remained there for nine months, experiencing all the horrors of a debtor's prison, until his good friend, Bernardo de Gálvez, was appointed captain general of Cuba in 1784. Not only did Gálvez release him from prison, but he also allowed him to leave the island and return to the United States. Eventually, the Commonwealth of Virginia repaid Pollock some of the sums owed him, and this enabled him to repay his creditors in New Orleans. By 1811, except for about $9,000, all of Pollock's debts had been canceled. While living with his daughter and son-in-law in Pinckneyville, Mississippi, the western financier of the American Revolution died in 1823. By then, all of his debts had long been paid.

The sculpture of Pollock's monumental head is the best-known work by adopted Baton Rouge sculptor Frank Hayden. It is a ten-foot bronze sculpture with a concrete pedestal, and it was completed in 1979. Since all of Mr. Pollock's portraits and papers were destroyed in the 1860s when the battleship USS *Essex* bombarded St. Francisville, this sculpture is not a true portrait of Pollock. Hayden said that he rendered an artistic interpretation, giving the face very piercing eyes and a wide-open mouth as if crying out or gasping for breath. The hair, or helmet, is stretched to include the nine

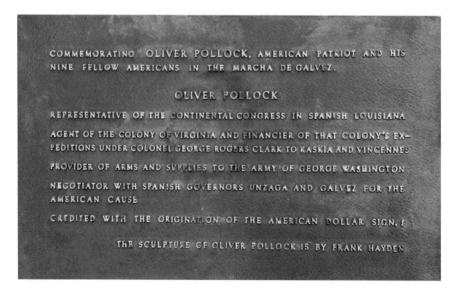

Plaque on Pollock's statue. *Photo by Layne Photography.*

loyal Americans who marched with him and Governor Gálvez. In profile, the nine figures seem to be held in an elongated hand. The contrast between the deep relief and surface etching is characteristic of the reverse side of the sculpture. This side, which seems to be hollowed out and resembles an enormous ear, is actually a waving flag with thirteen stars in the upper left-hand corner. Engraved between the stripes on the flag is a direct quote from Pollock: "I was deaf to every motive except an ardent appreciation of our righteous cause. I have a heart still ready to bear new sufferings and to make new sacrifices."

The plaque dedicating the monument is attached to the base of the sculpture. It reads as follows:

COMMEMORATING OLIVER POLLOCK, AMERICAN PATRIOT AND HIS NINE FELLOW AMERICANS IN THE MARCHA DE GALVEZ

OLIVER POLLOCK

REPRESENTATIVE OF THE CONTINENTAL CONGRESS IN SPANISH LOUISIANA AGENT OF THE COLONY OF VIRGINIA AND FINANCIER OF THAT COLONY'S EX-PEDITIONS UNDER COLONEL GEORGE ROGERS CLARK TO KASKIA AND VINCENNES

PROVIDER OF ARMS AND SUPPLIES TO THE ARMY OF GEORGE WASHINGTON

NEGOTIATOR WITH SPANISH GOVERNORS UNZAGA AND GALVEZ FOR THE AMERICAN CAUSE

CREDITED WITH THE ORIGINATION OF THE AMERICAN DOLLAR SIGN

THE SCULPTURE OF OLIVER POLLOCK IS BY FRANK HAYDEN

Part III

FAMOUS HISTORICAL MONUMENTS

OLD LOUISIANA STATE CAPITOL BUILDING

Mark Twain actually made fun of it, as he did of many things, labeling it a "little sham Castle" and a "monstrosity on the Mississippi." Yet in 1973, it was designated a National Historical Landmark, and a respected national magazine, the *American Architecture and Building News*, claimed that it was "assertive of independent characteristics."

The building's architect, James Harrison Dakin, endured both physical and legal battles over its construction. After it was built, within two separate twenty-four-hour periods, its interior was gutted by fire. Despite this, it still breaks spectacularly into the Baton Rouge skyline from its bluff overlooking the Mississippi River and dominates the intersection of North Boulevard and Riverside Mall in downtown Baton Rouge. It is none other than Louisiana's simultaneously venerated and maligned Old State Capitol Building.

This Gothic castle, reflected in the pool of the ultramodern Centroplex Building, is an anachronism—completely out of place within the confines of the time and space it occupies. When it was designed and completed late in 1849, however, it was very much in keeping with the architectural style of Gothic Revival that was experiencing its heyday then. The castellated Gothic structure was generally accepted and even considered "one of the finest buildings in the South" while being "exquisitely picturesque and subservient alike to utility and ornament." One contemporary critic, however, deviated from the norm and called the building "the most unsightly mass that ever was built for $250,000.00, and it is only fit for an insane asylum." It seems that had several problems, including a design flaw that resulted in the roof leaking during Louisiana's torrential rains, as well as an inadequate water supply. In addition, even though a skylight was located in the center of the statehouse, it failed to provide sufficient natural light. Since the interior of the building was always dark, gas lighting had to be installed in 1858. To make matters worse, although the first floor's large rotunda was intended to showcase a statue of George Washington, commissioned in 1850 to be sculpted by Hiram Power, it failed to materialize until 1859. Fortunately, by then, the small skylight above the rotunda had been enlarged to accommodate the openings of the second and third stories, increasing the amount of natural light not just to the first floor but to the second and third stories as well.

In 1852, the idea had been conceived to encircle this building with a cast-iron fence. Strongly believed to have been also designed by Dakin in Baton Rouge before his death, the fence is a combination of both Greek and Gothic motifs and political symbols. It was cast in Mr. John Hill's Baton Rouge foundry, which was located on Front Street (River Road) between North Street and the Pentagon Barracks and completed in 1855. The seven-foot-tall fence is an integral part of the historic building and surrounds it for about one-third of a mile. It is as distinctive as the winding iron stairway that sweeps up gracefully to the stained-glass dome.

Old State Capitol staircase. *Photo by Layne Photography.*

The trefoil and quatrefoil designs used in the architecture of the building are repeated in the 1,575-foot fence that later was placed on the Louisiana Preservation Alliance list of ten of the most endangered historic sites in the state. Originally the fence was bolted on the bottom only, slotted together and supported by its own weight. Each piece of the fence interlocks, which in turn makes a section between the posts. There are four gates, which are so heavy that they can only be opened by using supporting rollers. The posts on each side of the gates are topped by two large cast-iron eagles. Today, the fence rests on a concrete foundation and remains a classic example of pre–Civil War cast-iron work.

By 1859, the landscaping for the building had been completed. The terracing was finished, and all the trees, shrubs and flowers were flourishing. During the 1850s, when Henry Watkins Allen was a state legislator, he had actively worked to embellish the state grounds. During his previous extensive travels, Allen had purchased rare trees and shrubs for the express purpose of planting them here. The results of his labors were now highly visible.

Then came the Civil War, and Dakin's "magnificent castle" fell to Union troops and was alternately used as a barracks, a hospital and a prison. In December 1862, a cooking fire erupted twice and gutted the interior of the building. The sturdy outer walls, over which Dakin had labored so

Old State Capitol staircase from above. *Photo by Layne Photography.*

painstakingly, resisted the fiery ordeal and remained virtually untouched. For the next twenty years, though, the building was left to rack and ruin.

The end of carpetbagger rule brought the restoration of Baton Rouge's capitol on the Mississippi. In 1880, Governor Louis Alfred Wiltz appointed William Freret to restore the building. The New Orleans architect retained the basic outer structure, adding a fourth story and a new, larger entrance that provided more natural light. Inside, he made his most significant contribution to the reconstruction by using the iron spiral staircase, reputably fashioned originally for Mexico's Emperor Maximilian, and creating the kaleidoscopic stained-glass dome. Unfortunately, in 1882, Freret decided to gild the outer lily by placing traceried iron turrets on top of the four main towers and adding bartizan turrets at every upper corner. The latter proved too much "Gothicizing" not only for Mark Twain but also for the citizens of Louisiana. Especially

Old State Capitol staircase with dome. *Photo by Layne Photography.*

Old State Capitol staircase, another view. *Photo by Layne Photography.*

after the Civil War, they had wanted everything, particularly their capitol building, restored to its previous state to serve as a reminder of the chivalry and gentility of antebellum times. The new turrets proved so unpopular that they were removed in 1915, thus retaining Dakin's original architectural lines.

In 1931, Louisiana's new skyscraper capitol was completed, and the Old State Capitol was vacated of its legislative contents. Today, its walls echo only with the sounds of tourists and the staff members of several state and local agencies. But standing at the foot of the spiral staircase, looking up at what resembles a "huge, stained glass umbrella," it is impossible to forget that these same walls once reverberated with impassioned political oratory, particularly during the unsuccessful impeachment trial of Huey P. Long. It is also impossible to ignore the debt of gratitude owed to James Dakin for his insistence on quality construction, which has enabled this building to survive and withstand the repairs and renovations that have occurred every ten years. Since 1932, when the legislature moved to the opposite end of Baton Rouge's downtown Third Street, the Old State Capitol has been used mainly for the purpose of creating more office space for state workers. It is also used for gala receptions, debutante balls and weddings. During one

LANDMARKS AND MONUMENTS OF BATON ROUGE

of the later restorations between 1991 and 1993 under Governor Charles Elson "Buddy" Roemer, the architect in charge, Eean McNaughton, stated, "There is no other building like it in the United States. It is a jewel worthy of the preservation effort. There are other buildings in this style, but there isn't another one that incorporates the stained glass and cast-iron."

Whether it is considered Baton Rouge's "magnificent obsession" or "magnificent folly," the Old State Capitol remains the one local monument that simply cannot be ignored. In other states in the Union, the idea of "marrying Xanadu to Westminster Abbey" is difficult to understand or even comprehend. They forget that nineteenth-century citizens of Louisiana never built public buildings for just one purpose and never strictly for civic ceremony, either. They built to please their aesthetic sense. The same may be applied to and said about its cast-iron fence. It, too, survived attempted demolitions, repairs and renovations dating from the 1930s until the summer of 2008, when the general contractor Cangelosi-Ward completed the most recent restoration. The architect with this firm, Jerry Campbell, emphatically stated, "There is not another one that exists like this one, to our knowledge, in the country." Whether painted a shiny black or a dark green, the cast-iron fence is generally considered an engineering marvel. It goes hand and glove with the building itself.

MERCI TRAIN, OR FRENCH GRATITUDE TRAIN

There is a rather unusual "monument" on the northeast corner of the Old State Capitol grounds. Beneath a lovely pavilion sits a World War I vintage French train, one out of the forty-nine that the French people sent to the people of the United States after the end of World War II. Each of the existing forty-eight states was to receive one of the cars, leaving the forty-ninth car to be shared by Hawaii and the District of Colombia. The idea to send the surplus old boxcars originated with a French World War I veteran and railroad worker named André Picard. He spearheaded a movement to send a tangible expression of gratitude from the people of France to the people of the United States for the invaluable aid given to them in their time of dire need during and after World War II. There are thirty-nine of these boxcars still on display throughout the United States, and one of them is here in Baton Rouge, Louisiana.

Following World War II, after years of war and occupation by the Nazis, France was in ruins and finding it difficult to return to any semblance of

Merci Train on the Old State Capitol grounds. *Photo by Layne Photography.*

order. Aware of the predicament of the French people, New York radio personality Drew Pearson wanted to come to their aid without involving the governments of the two countries. He strongly believed that having people-to-people friendships between nations was the only way to establish a lasting world peace. So, he organized a drive whereby the American people filled seven hundred boxcars with food, clothing, fuel, medicine and other relief supplies and sent them to the devastated Europeans in what they termed the Friendship Trains. These boxcars sailed on board ships from New York and arrived in France on December 18, 1947.

A little over a year later, the French responded to this kindness by sending their *Merci* Trains to the United States. They arrived in New York Harbor on February 3, 1949. The donations came from more than 6 million citizens of France. Among the items the French selected were finely costumed dolls, costumes from the various provinces, statues, articles of clothing such as fine lingerie with lace, furniture, household ornaments such as vases and crystal and even a Legion of Honour Medal alleged to have belonged to Napoleon.

In 1949, Governor Earl K. Long, brother of former Governor Huey P. Long, received the boxcar sent to Baton Rouge, Louisiana. This boxcar had ridden the Rock Island Railroad from Jackson, Mississippi, on February 12 and arrived in New Orleans on February 13 at 6:00 a.m. It was displayed

Merci Train, with the
Old State Capitol in the
background. *Photo by Layne
Photography.*

there for several days and then sent to Baton Rouge. French Consul General
Lionel Vasse had the honor of presenting the railway car, loaded with gifts
from the French people from all walks of life.

As on the other forty-eight trains, this boxcar that was sent to Louisiana
was marked with the symbol of the *Merci* Train—a circular plaque with a
frontal view of a steam engine adorned with flowers symbolic of Flanders
Field, where so many American soldiers were buried during World War I.
The other plaques on the boxcar represent each one of the provinces that
existed and participated at that time, evidencing that each province had a
flag or coat of arms similar to our state flags.

There are two separate markers relating the history of the boxcar. The
first one states:

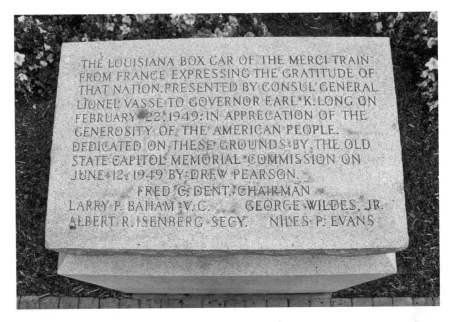

Plaque (close-up) giving historical information about the *Merci* Train. *Photo by Layne Photography.*

Boxcar used in the 1ˢᵗ World War presented by the French
National Railroads to the state of LOUISIANA in gratitude for the
Help given to France by the American people.

The second, a granite marker, declares:

THE LOUISIANA BOXCAR OF "THE MERCI TRAIN"
FROM FRANCE EXPRESSING THE GRATITUDE OF
THAT NATION. PRESENTED BY CONSUL GENERAL
LIONEL VASSE TO GOVERNOR EARL K. LONG ON
FEBRUARY 22, 1949. IN APPRECIATION OF THE
GENEROSITY OF THE AMERICAN PEOPLE.
DEDICATED ON THESE GROUNDS BY THE OLD
STATE CAPITOL MEMORIAL COMMISSION ON
JUNE 12, 1949 BY DREW PEARSON.
FRED C. DENT—CHAIRMAN.
LARRY P. BAHAM—V.C.   GEORGE WILDES, JR.
ALBERT R. ISENBERG, SECY.   NILES P. EVANS

NEW LOUISIANA STATE CAPITOL BUILDING

How does one describe and/or categorize the grandiose New State Capitol Building of Louisiana? It was the realization of the dream held by Louisiana's most controversial, colorful governor, Huey Pierce Long, who had the bravado and drive to ramrod his vision for the building. He wanted to break from the tradition of erecting domed edifices for the state capitol buildings. He succeeded. He wanted it to bring the skyscraper mentality, in vogue in the 1930s, to the state of Louisiana. He succeeded. He wanted it to reflect the varied ethnic backgrounds, the diverse agricultural and business interests and the intellectual and cultural facets of the state. He succeeded. To accomplish this end, he and his advisory panels assembled the most talented group of architects, sculptors, painters and artisans available. He needed men with vision to implement what he saw in his mind's eye for the people of Louisiana. Through the construction of this building, he wanted the state to be seen and heard.

New State Capitol, August 1999. *Photo by Zozaya.*

Sometimes referred to as the most beautiful statehouse in the nation, it remains the tallest capitol building in the United States. It has thirty-four stories and is 450 feet in height. It was built on the site of the old Louisiana State University campus. It was commissioned to be built in January 1931 and was completed in March 1932 at a cost of $5 million. The towering building, which can be seen from every angle for miles, is a perfect example of how a community's monuments reflect the prevailing values and culture. This classic Art Deco showcase made a political statement that cannot be compared to any other statement made in a state capitol building in the United

States. It heralded political and economic change in the South, and it was a tangible testament to populism and to forgetting the culture of the Old Plantation South. It became a symbol of looking to the future, surviving the Great Depression and resolving to confront and master the challenges of the twentieth century. From its lofty exterior to within its walls, it also managed to capture the essence of the state's diverse political character.

The New State Capitol Building was the dream of Louisiana's forty-first governor, Huey Pierce Long, who was elected to office in 1928 and served as Louisiana's governor until 1932. The new governor could easily afford to give in to his grandiose building ideas without regard to the expense. The economically depressed state was in the throes of the Great Depression, and highly skilled labor was available for fifty to seventy-five cents per hour. Governor Long personally selected the prestigious New Orleans architectural firm of Weiss, Dreyfous and Seiferth to design the building and instructed it to build a tower that would be visible from "all points" and depict the history of the state—and to do it quickly. His directions were followed, and the building, with its exterior of Alabama limestone, was completed in just fourteen months. Of course, this was with the cooperation and assistance of the contracting firm of George A. Fuller Company of Washington, D.C., also personally selected by Long himself, whose previous works included the Lincoln Memorial and the Flatiron Building in New York City.

This Capitol Building rises from the highest elevation of a plateau of land that is fifty feet above the low-water level of the Mississippi River. There, within the twenty-seven acres of beautifully landscaped grounds, it is set in a formal plaza, with all the surrounding sites grading up to it. The building is approached from the main entrance by ascending a flight of broad steps made of Minnesota granite, broken by platforms. The lowest flight of steps consists of thirteen steps, one for each one of the original colonies. On each side of these flights of steps is a series of stepped buttresses adorned with pelicans (the state bird) and the American lotus (a plant indigenous to the marshes of Louisiana). At the topmost buttresses are groups of statuary, carved from Indiana limestone with similar compositions. The group on the left, or west, represents the Louisiana pioneers. These were the Spanish and French explorers and colonists of the seventeenth and eighteenth centuries. The group on the right, or east, representing the Patriots, is a memorial to the heterogeneous citizens of Louisiana who fought and died to defend their state, country and liberties. The famous *Sorrows of War* is within the Patriots group—mother and father, widow and orphan.

Pioneers statuary group. *Photo by Zozaya.*

These epic statuary groups were the creation of sculptor Lorado Taft. The remaining thirty-five steps were arranged in four groups, each inscribed with the states' names in the order of their admission to the Union. The top step is carved with the inscription "E Pluribus Unum." The portals around the entrance doors are decorated with reliefs that reveal Louisiana's economy and resources. Over these doors, two eagles flank the state seal with the pelican, while above the eagles stand six statues with the coat of arms of the entities that have governed Louisiana—Indians, who were the original inhabitants, and four central figures representing Spain, France, the United States and the Confederacy.

The striking Memorial Hall features a large bronze relief map showing many of the state's products, encircled with the names of the sixty-four parishes. Sculptures of some of Louisiana's governors that are twice as large as life-sized stand in this hall: Pierre Le Moyne Sieur d'Iberville, first colonial governor; William C.C. Claiborne, first American governor; Henry Watkins Allen, the Confederate governor; and P.B.S. Pinchback, first black governor of the state.

The wings of the base contain the two houses of the state legislature: the Senate on the west and the House of Representatives on the east. Both chambers can be reached through spectacular bronze doors. The panels on the House doors represent the state's history, while the panels on the Senate door depict the colonial history. The first floor of the northern side of the base was originally occupied by executive offices of the governor, lieutenant governor and Speaker of the House. The second floor housed conference and hearing rooms, while the third floor provided rooms for more offices.

The set-back base held the judiciary branch on the fourth and fifth floors. Before this branch of government was removed from the Capitol Building altogether, the floors contained two courtrooms, a law library and offices for judges and clerks. Today, one of the former courtrooms is the governor's pressroom and the other one is used for office space, while the original law library is in the governor's suite of offices.

From this massive substantial base and its flanking wings arose the towering shaft that symbolically reached out to the heavens and interrupted the Baton Rouge skyline. The first break as the square tower rises is at the twenty-second story. At this point, four allegorical winged figures guard corners, representing Law, Science, Philosophy and Art. The next break comes on the twenty-seventh floor, with an Observation Deck at a height of 350 feet, followed by another story, totaling twenty-eight stories of limestone and marble. In its entirety, the Capitol Building displays more than thirty varieties of marble and stone, representing every state that produced marble, as well as several foreign countries. The colors vary from Italian dark red marble, brecciated with white, to violet French marble, a rose marble from Spain and black marble from the Pyrenees Mountains veined with white and with rose and yellow markings. Red and yellow

The author and three of her children in front of the New State Capitol in 1962. *Photo by Walter R. Krousel Jr.*

mottled stone from Greece is used on the fourth floor. There are corridors of gray and white marble from Alabama and blue-green marble pilasters from the Green Mountains of Vermont. It appears that the architect and builder needed to use a profusion of color to contrast vividly with the gray limestone of the exterior.

Bronze is used extensively throughout the building. Beginning with the entrance portal and continuing to the four sets of doors leading from the Memorial Hall to the House and Senate chambers, bronze continues to be used for the three elevator entrances. All of the plaques, medallions, doorknobs, grillwork, patterned hardwood floors and magnificent friezes were made using this alloy without any regard for costs. Nowhere is this more apparent than in Memorial Hall, which is 35 by 120 feet and two stories high. As the main public space for the building, it presents a grand entrance. This is emphasized by the portraits of great men prominent in Louisiana history that are displayed on the exterior walls of the House and Senate chambers.

Some of the murals and frescoes that decorated the building were designed and executed by the nationally known Jules Guerin, who had painted the murals for the Old Pennsylvania Station in New York, the Lincoln Memorial and the Chicago Civic Opera House, to name a few. Others were painted by Conrad Albrizio, who had studied fresco painting in France and Italy. Unfortunately, some of his frescoes did not survive the years of neglect.

Sculptures abound throughout the building. From the epic statuary groups to the sculptured heads on the relief panels and the free-standing figures, the sculptors were all selected by the architects based on their reputations. Lorado Taft and Lee Lawrie were the foremost architectural sculptors in the Union. Adolph A. Weinman and Ulric Ellerhusen were also prominent sculptors who used their talents in the capitol building. Last but not least, there were quite a few lesser-known New Orleans sculptors, such as Angela Gregory, Albert Rieker, Juanita Gonzales, John Lachin and Rudolph Parducci, who contributed by using their considerable skills.

For sixteen floors, the building's tower rises without outside adornments. From the twenty-second to the twenty-fifth floors, the exterior erupts in bands of ornamentation. The twenty-sixth floor is undecorated. From the twenty-fourth floor, there is a small elevator that goes up to the thirtieth floor. From that point, there are three flights of steps leading up to the observation tower, from where it is possible to see much of downtown Baton Rouge, including the Mississippi River.

Unfortunately, there was a period of about fifty years when the historical, artistic and cultural importance of the New State Capitol was ignored. Perhaps it was as the architect, Solis Seiferth, stated in his preface to the book *The Louisiana Capitol, Its Art and Architecture* by Vincent F. Kubly:

> *The involved literary and symbolic content of the capitol's decoration, intended to embody the noblest of human values and aspirations for the instruction and enlightenment of future generations, is largely unintelligible, and few make the effort to decipher the building's message and meaning.*

Also contributing to the losses was the deeply rooted antipathy of many to Huey P. Long and his political philosophy. There was also a desire for a contemporary style accompanied by a reaction against the Art Deco style. Whatever the case may be, the lack of supervised maintenance of the building resulted in the loss of thousands of valuable artifacts, such as solid-brass doorknobs, and led to innumerable crimes against history, architecture and art.

The proliferation of architectural and artistic detail in this structure can overwhelm one's appreciation and evaluation of the capitol's symbolic distinction and its historic significance. However, it should not dull the acknowledgement, recognition and appreciation of the sense of accomplishment and pride that the people of Louisiana gained from its towering, magnificent state capitol building. It cannot belie the heated, passionate oratory and political maneuverings that were ongoing in its chambers, halls and suites. It cannot ignore the fact that the man responsible for its construction, Huey Pierce Long, was shot within its walls, as attested to by a plaque on the first floor of the building marking the place on the wall of the executive corridor where it occurred.

Louisiana's New State Capitol, while an architectural oddity because it is a governmental center that has been outgrown, remains nationally and internationally recognized for its artistic importance. It is still considered one of the best examples of the Beaux Arts architectural tradition in the Union. The number of artists and stylistic modes points to the building's importance as a showpiece of the last phase of the Renaissance tradition in American architecture, according to Kubly. With the revival of the Art Deco architectural style, it can reclaim its significance in this art form. Perhaps Solis Seiferth, its architect, was more than justified when he wrote, quoting Robert Livingston, "We have lived long but this is the noblest work of our whole lives." This quotation is chiseled in stone beside the fifty-foot-high main entrance.

LIBERTY BELL

Sitting on the grounds of the Old Arsenal Building, in the shadow of Louisiana's towering New State Capitol Building, this replica of the Liberty Bell invites an inevitable comparison between the old and the new. Maybe it serves as a reminder that we should remember the past as we address the needs of the present and the future.

Louisiana's Liberty Bell was brought from New Orleans to Baton Rouge and mounted here permanently as late as 1972. Originally securely mounted in headstock and frame, it arrived in New Orleans on May 25, 1950. Subsequently, the replica of the Liberty Bell was shipped to Baton Rouge for presentation. It was accepted on behalf of the State of Louisiana on the state capitol's steps in a ceremony presided over by Lieutenant Governor William J. Dodd on July 6, 1950. The Liberty Bell given to Louisiana on that July 6 was a replica of the original bell that had been mounted in Philadelphia, Pennsylvania, in 1752, except for the fact that the crack had been painted on this bell to represent the original without interfering with the bell's ability to ring.

Shortly afterward, the bell was shipped back to New Orleans, for its intended and permanent home was to be in the *Cabildo*, which had been the seat of the Spanish colonial government. This seemed logical because the bell had first arrived in New Orleans on May 25, 1950, to much fanfare, and Archbishop Joseph Francis Rummel requested that all Catholic churches in the city toll their bells in jubilation at 11:00 a.m. on that day. Arrangements were already being been made for a second presentation and acceptance ceremony at the *Cabildo* the following Monday, July 10, 1950. Speed seemed to be of the essence since presentation in most other states had been made on July 4, 1950.

In 1950, six copper firms in the United States ordered and financed two-thousand-pound replicas of the original Liberty Bell. That same year, as part of a Savings Bond Drive with the slogan "Save for Your Independence," the United States Treasury Department ordered fifty-five full-sized replicas to be cast—one for each state, the District of Columbia and the territories. The government distributed the bells to each location to gain support for the bond drive. It had selected the Paccard Foundry in Annecy-le-Vieux, France, to cast the bells and then ship them as gifts to the states and territories of the United States, as well as the District of Columbia. This foundry had been selected because of its reputation as skilled bell makers, descended from generations of experts in their craft who used the traditional materials

Liberty Bell. *Photo by Layne Photography.*

and original formulas to cast their bells. From the minute when more than a ton of copper alloy was poured over the first rough mold, Monsieur Henri Paccard, whose great-grandfather had started the company in 1794, supervised the work of his artisans during each step in the process until the final delicate tuning. Wax molds of the letters on the original bell were hand-carved and appear on each replica, announcing:

> *Proclaim liberty throughout the land*
> *Unto all the inhabitants thereof,*
> *By order of the assembly of the province of Pennsylvania.*

The cost of the bells was unknown at the time because they were a complimentary gift from the American copper industry to the government of the United States. It seems that the only stipulation for the use of these bells was that they were to be appropriately displayed and rung on special patriotic occasions.

It was during this Savings Bond Drive that the Liberty Bell replica was taken from New Orleans, supposedly on a six-week tour, and displayed in twenty-two cities in Louisiana. When the tour was completed, this replica, the thirty-ninth in the series, was returned to Baton Rouge and placed unostentatiously on the grounds of the Old Arsenal Museum in 1972.

The history of the original iconic Liberty Bell dates back to early in 1752 when the Pennsylvania Provincial Assembly commissioned its London agent, Robert Charles, to procure the London firm of Lester and Pack, currently the Whitechapel Bell Foundry, to cast the bell. The city bell, said to have been brought by founder William Penn, was no longer of the quality needed to be heard at a greater distance in the rapidly expanding city, so they ordered a bell that weighed about two thousand pounds. Instructions to the foundry also requested that the bell be cast by its best workmen and examined carefully before shipping. During our nation's early years, these bells were an absolute necessity to summon lawmakers to legislative sessions, call citizens to public meetings and alert them to important proclamations. Because their functions were so important to the communities and sometimes invaluable to the safety of their citizens, the bells had to be of the highest quality.

When the Liberty Bell arrived in Philadelphia in August 1752, it was immediately mounted on a stand to test its sound. Unfortunately, at the first ring of the clapper, the rim of the bell cracked. The stories abounded then about how the bell, made in England, had to be recast in America before it could ring proclaiming freedom. Two local artisans, John Pass and John Stow, volunteered to recast the bell, even though they were inexperienced in this trade. At Stow's foundry the bell was shattered, melted down and molded into a new bell. This occurred only after Mr. Pass used the expertise he had acquired working in a factory in Malta to augment the metal by using 10 percent copper in the alloy mixture. The brittleness of the bell had been tamed, and the new bell was presented for use in March 1753. When the bell was struck, however, though it did not break, it produced such a terrible sound that Pass and Stow took the bell away and recast it again. Their renewed efforts brought forth a new bell in June 1753. The sound was more acceptable, and the bell was hung in the steeple of the Pennsylvania Statehouse that same month.

From this point forward, the history of the Liberty Bell takes on a checkered path with varied and sometimes conflicting facts and often with highly romanticized spins to the story. One of these versions states that when bells were rung when the Declaration of Independence was read in July 1776, the Liberty Bell was one of the bells ringing. Although there are no contemporary accounts confirming this, historians still believe that it was one of the bells rung. The thirty-ninth replica of the bell, mounted on the Baton Rouge State Capital grounds, embodies all this history.

The City of Philadelphia, which owns the Liberty Bell, has allowed it to travel to expositions and patriotic gatherings. Huge crowds have met the bell whenever and wherever it went. Naturally, additional cracking has taken place, and souvenir hunters have chipped away pieces. In 1915, Philadelphia refused to let the bell travel anymore. After World War II, the city allowed the National Park Service to take custody of the bell but insisted on retaining its ownership. In 1976, it was moved from its home in Independence Hall to a nearby glass pavilion. This was followed by another move in 2003, when the bell was moved to the larger Liberty Bell Center adjacent to the pavilion. What becomes very clear, throughout all the traveling and changes of location, is the fact that since the American Revolution in 1776 and immediately prior, this bell has always been a tangible symbol of a people's right within their legitimate governmental structure to the pursuit of freedom. In the United States, the Liberty Bell is almost venerated.

GÁLVEZ PLAZA

At a period of time in the 1770s and earlier when the Spanish, French, English and American colonists were struggling to gain and maintain control of the lower Mississippi River and the Gulf of Mexico, supremacy over the "Spanish Borderlands" was of the essence. Spanish Louisiana was extremely fortunate then to have Don Bernardo de Gálvez as its governor. After Spain declared war on England on May 8, 1779, he led a small heterogeneous army and captured British Fort Richmond on September 21, 1779, renaming it Fort San Carlos. This first Battle of Baton Rouge, the only Revolutionary War battle fought and won outside the original thirteen colonies, qualified citizens of Baton Rouge and the state of Louisiana to be Sons and Daughters of the American Revolution. Therefore, it stands to reason that Baton Rouge, although belatedly, would design a memorial in its downtown area paying tribute to Gálvez.

Gálvez Plaza in downtown Baton Rouge was built and developed to celebrate the 200th anniversary of the Battle of Baton Rouge, which occurred during the American Revolutionary War in 1779. It was the creation of the Baton Rouge Bicentennial Commission and the Baton Rouge Civic Center Plaza Committee, which had insisted that a commemoration of

View of Gálvez Plaza from the north side. *Photo by Layne Photography.*

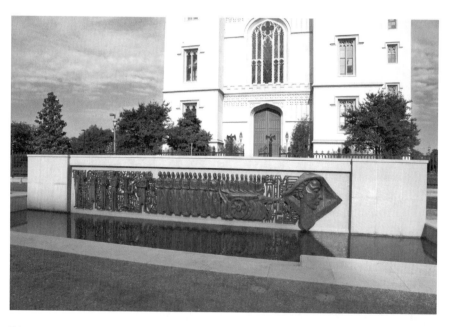

Frieze on the wall in front of the Gálvez Plaza fountain. *Photo by Layne Photography.*

the American Revolution be included in the Civic Center adjacent to the courthouse. There, across from the Old State Capitol Building and between it and the new Parish Library, space was assigned for the plaza. A fountain at one end anchors the plaza, with a wall as a backdrop that is about four feet tall. On one side of the low wall, there is a thirty-foot-long bronze frieze depicting the Marcha de Gálvez by Baton Rouge sculptor Frank Hayden. The other side features three plaques.

One is a bronze plaque entitled "The Capture of Baton Rouge by Gálvez, 1779," and it is "dedicated to the memory of Erich Sternberg, Goudchaux's, Inc., September, 1979." It was made from a 1976 bicentennial lithograph by Sigmund Abeles. The second is also a bronze plaque honoring Governor Bernardo de Gálvez and his achievements. It reads:

Marcha de Galvez

Near This Site in September 1779, Under the Leadership of Governor Bernardo de Galvez and His Aide Oliver Pollock, Spanish Regulars, Americans and Louisiana Militiamen Marched from New Orleans to Baton Rouge to Engage the British Forces at Fort New Richmond. Their Victory Destroyed British Hopes of Capturing New Orleans and Controlling the Mississippi River.

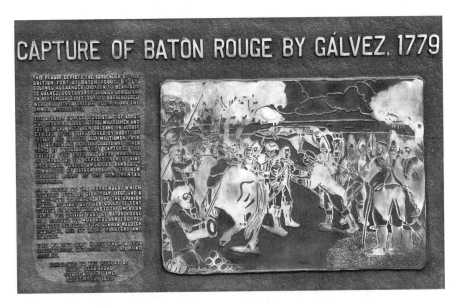

Plaque depicting the capture of Baton Rouge, 1779. *Photo by Layne Photography.*

These passages are incorporated into the sculpture:

"WHAT MORTAL OR GOD COMES HERE IN HIS RAGE,
TO TROUBLE THE GENTLE PEACE OF MY HAPPY BANKS
TO FOLLOW ME, YOU LEFT YOUR FIELDS,
YOUR LOVING CHILDREN, AND FAITHFUL WIVES...
BRAVE WARRIORS, COMPANIONS OF MY GLORY,
IT WAS WITH YOUR HANDS, TODAY, THAT I WON MY VICTORY."

"THE CAPTURE OF THE BLUFF AT BATON ROUGE BY HIS LORDSHIP GALVEZ"
JULIAN POYDRAS, 1779

Speaking of the Battle of Baton Rouge, Bernardo de Gálvez bid farewell to the people at the end of his term of office:

"IT WILL ALWAYS BE AN INCONTESTABLE PROOF OF YOUR LOVE FOR ME AND PUBLIC TESTIMONY OF MY GOOD CONDUCT TOWARDS YOU."
BERNARDO DE GALVEZ, 1783

THE BRONZE RELIEF IS BY FRANK HAYDEN

Gálvez Plaza plaque detailing his achievements. *Photo by Layne Photography.*

70

The third marker features a Louisiana Purchase Bicentennial (1803–2003) plaque, "A Patriot's Legacy," honoring the Patriots of the American Revolution led by General Bernardo de Gálvez, governor of Louisiana, and presented by the Louisiana Society Children of the American Revolution, the Louisiana Society Daughters of the American Revolution and the Louisiana Society Sons of the American Revolution. Its bronze marker reads:

Dedicated to the
Fourth Governor of Spanish Louisiana, 1776–1783
Benefactor of the American colonies during the American Revolution
Victor over the British in West Florida at the Battles of:
Manchac   Pensacola   Mobile   Baton Rouge
Loved, Respected and Held in Grateful Memory

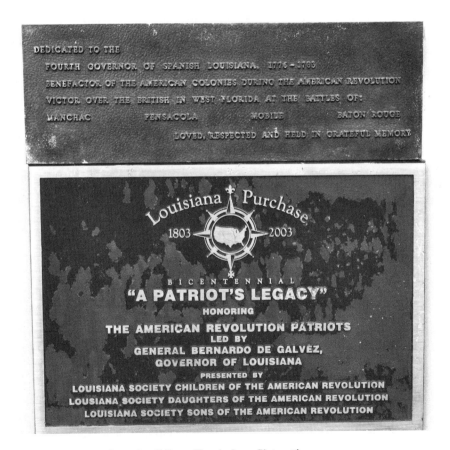

Bicentennial plaque honoring Gálvez. *Photo by Layne Photography.*

At the other end of the plaza, resting on its tall pedestal, is the monument dedicated to Oliver Pollock overlooking the fountain.

The force responsible for this belated memorial was born in Málaga, Spain, in 1748. Don Gálvez could easily be called one of the darlings of history. He had already established himself as a brilliant civil and military leader in Spain and its colonies when he became the fourth Spanish governor to Louisiana on January 1, 1777. As one of the most popular colonial governors ever in the state of Louisiana, he was described by Louisiana historian Charles Gayarré in his *Romance of the History of Louisiana* as possessing that "nobleness of mien, that gracefulness of manner, that dignified and at the same time easy affability for high and low, which in persons of his rank, never fails to win the heart." All of these qualities that he possessed, both military genius and social skills, joined together, enabling him to accomplish an almost impossible feat: enlisting and uniting heterogeneous groups to form a military unit ready to fight for the Spanish against the British.

First, he had to dispel the fears of the Hispanophobe French Creoles who still remembered Spanish Governor Alejandro O'Reilly's bloody execution of their leaders after the failed Revolt of 1768 against former Spanish Governor Don Antonio de Ulloa. He also had to assemble, with Oliver Pollock's help, whatever military resources were available to outfit his militia and navy. The naval forces were seriously impeded from action when a hurricane in August 1779 destroyed most of the ships. Several weeks later, "late summer fevers" struck and further decimated the unit. Somehow, Gálvez overcame all these factors, left New Orleans and marched onward to Fort Richmond in Baton Rouge. He assembled and led a force that consisted of 520 regulars, about two-thirds of whom were recent recruits from Mexico and the Canary Islands; 60 militiamen; 80 free blacks and mulattoes; and 10 American volunteers headed by Oliver Pollock, Gálvez's aide-de-camp. On their march up the Mississippi River, his force grew by another 600 men, including Indians and Acadians. At its peak, the unit grew and numbered more than 1,400 men. By the time they reached Fort Bute, the hardships of the march had reduced the number by several hundred. On September 7, 1779, Gálvez successfully attacked the token force there in Fort Bute and emerged victorious.

After resting for several days, Gálvez and his men marched the fifteen miles to Baton Rouge and arrived on September 12. There, Gálvez and his military units were confronted by a well-fortified garrison that cloistered more than 400 regular army troops and 150 militia, all under the command of

Lieutenant Colonel Alexander Dickson. These army troops were composed of British army regulars from the Sixteenth and Sixtieth Regiments, some artillerymen and several companies of Germans from the Third Waldeck Regiment. Lieutenant Colonel Dickson had recognized early on that Fort Bute was indefensible and had correspondingly sheltered most of his troops in Baton Rouge. He had also directed the construction of Fort Richmond, an earthen bulwark with spiked obstacles on the outside. This, in turn, was surrounded by a moat that was eighteen feet wide and nine feet deep. Thirteen cannons completed the fortification.

Faced with this reality, Don Gálvez devised a battle plan, different from his original one. Recognizing that a frontal attack on the fort would take too much of a toll on lives and property, he orchestrated a brilliant fake attack. Since the most logical point for assault seemed to be from a small thicket of trees in front of the fort, Gálvez sent a detachment of his poorly trained militia to create disturbances there, with specific orders to cut down trees, making as much noise as possible. The British were foiled by this ruse and unleashed massed volleys of grapeshot at the detachment.

While the British commandant was occupied with this maneuver, Gálvez and his men dug siege trenches, establishing secure gun pits within firing range of the fort, in an orchard directly opposite and across from the fort. They placed their artillery pieces in these gun pits and opened fire against the British on September 21, 1779. Within three and a half hours of this barrage, on September 22, 1779, Lieutenant Colonel Alexander Dickson surrendered his British forces there to Gálvez. Ford Richmond was then renamed Fort San Carlos in honor of the Spanish monarch. Don Bernardo de Gálvez demanded and was granted terms that included the surrender of the 80 regular infantrymen at Fort Panmure, modern-day Natchez, Mississippi. The next day, Dickson surrendered 375 regular troops and was forced to dismantle his militia and send them home. Thus ended the first Battle of Baton Rouge, with the Spanish forces reporting only 3 casualties. The Spanish governor then sent a detachment of 50 men to secure control of Fort Panmure and dismissed his own militia companies. Leaving a sizable garrison in Baton Rouge, he returned to New Orleans with about 50 men.

Two hundred years later, Gálvez Plaza was dedicated on September 21, 1979, to honor the third Spanish governor of Louisiana. It was a gala occasion attended by the Spanish ambassador. Gifts were received from Juan Carlos, king of Spain, and among these gifts were carpets memorializing Don Bernardo de Gálvez. These are in storage now but will soon hang in the Baton Rouge Room of the renovated River Center Library.

Part IV

FAMOUS MILITARY
MONUMENTS

OLD ARSENAL

As one of the oldest landmarks in Baton Rouge, the Old Arsenal sits on a mound east of the New Louisiana State Capitol Building surrounded by a ten-foot brick wall. On a mound to the side of the arsenal, there is a cannon that still points to the Mississippi River. The compound has an aura of aloof silence, yet its mere presence seems to be a sharp contrast to the Capitol Building's modern skyscraper image. It is as if it had been selected to serve as a proud and perpetual link between the present and Baton Rouge's checkered past.

The need for safety and protection in the Baton Rouge area helps explain the magnificent construction of this building. Enclosed by the high brick wall, the rectangular-shaped arsenal has walls that are fifty-four inches thick, fashioned from hand-laid bricks overlaid with plaster. These walls are roofed by four-foot-thick slate shingles and floored by cypress planks. There are only five windows, which are heavily barred, and there are no gun holes. The air vents are so strategically placed that it would be impossible for a stray bullet to enter. The threshold is marked by a heavy timber door, barred with iron strips that replaced the original massive iron gates.

For more than a century, fantasy veiled the origins of the timeworn structure. Myths and legends about its construction and purpose spun off as freely and elaborately as the vines that once covered its walls. Some reports credited the French with building this edifice, while others claimed that the Spanish had designed it in the late seventeenth century. There was even

Old Arsenal Museum. *Photo by Layne Photography.*

considerable speculation as to whether it had been used as an arsenal at all. In fact, as late as 1956, a local newspaper account proposed that whether or not the building was an arsenal, there could be no doubt that it was "very old, of Spanish construction, and is probably one of the oldest buildings in Baton Rouge, if not the oldest."

A few sources periodically interjected the suggestion that the building had been erected by the United States government in the nineteenth century. However, the architecture of the depository and the romanticism with which the building had been endowed joined forces to reject this thought. To begin with, the arsenal overlooks Capitol Lake, formerly known as Bayou Grasse in honor of one of Baton Rouge's earliest and wealthiest Spanish settlers. The main, long room had a trapdoor leading into a cellar from which other tunnels, now sealed, led to other buildings in the garrison. Then the interior of the building, with its rows of pillars that support the beautifully arched ceiling, creating a perfect symmetry, definitely reflects Spanish structural design. It seemed logical to call the armory the Old Spanish Fort or the Old Spanish Arsenal.

Another school of thought theorized that the Old Arsenal was the last in a string of buildings that had composed Fort Richmond, built by the English in 1763 after they took over West Florida. At that time, it was a dirt fort on the banks of the Mississippi River, with its western end on present-day Boyd Street. The entrance was guarded by a heavy cast-iron door, which was the customary fashion of the time.

In 1779, the Spanish governor of Louisiana, Don Bernardo de Gálvez, captured Fort Richmond from the British and renamed it Fort San Carlos. For many, the arsenal became a monument to this battle.

Thirty-one years later, in 1810, Louisiana's geographic neighbor, West Florida, revolted against Spain, led by General Philemon Thomas. He seized Fort San Carlos and ousted the Spanish forces. The Spanish flag was supplanted by West Florida Republic's blue flag with a silver star. It flew over the fort until it was replaced by the Stars and Stripes banner, which was raised by United States regulars under Colonel Leonard Covington.

Contrary to the various visionary deductions expounded, historical research in the late 1960s revealed that the arsenal had been built in 1835 as the Third Powder Magazine for the United States Army. Possibly this magazine was a replacement or an addition to the Baton Rouge Military Cantonment and Arsenal, which, along with the famed Pentagon Barracks, had been started by the United States Army Corps of Engineers in May 1819.

For thirty-four years, this Third Powder Magazine was constantly used to supply ammunition to Louisiana forts. In the 1840s, its strategic location made it a principal provider for the United States Army in both the Seminole and Mexican-American Wars. For this purpose, the Old Arsenal and its Baton Rouge location on the Mississippi River was invaluable both for shipping and from a military standpoint.

When Louisiana captured this military post and joined the Confederacy in 1861, the contents of the magazine were used to supply Confederate armies in a dozen states. Within sixteen months, however, the Union forces had recaptured Baton Rouge. The arsenal was then used as a depot for the Northern armies of the Union until the end of the Civil War.

In 1869, following the Civil War, all munitions and machinery were stripped from the magazine and other arsenal buildings. It was then that the Military Cantonment was annexed to the Pentagon Barracks as the Baton Rouge Barracks. All of this property was transferred in 1886 to Louisiana State University. The old magazine building was quickly converted to a storehouse for library materials. When the university moved to its present location, the Louisiana State Police utilized the Old Arsenal building as a storehouse and a pistol firing range. After this, the Old Armory was left to deteriorate and slowly sunk to the lowly state of being nothing more than a repository for years of accumulated junk from the New State Capitol Building.

Fortunately, countless local citizens over the years, as attested to by the generations of Baton Rouge citizens who have scrawled their names on the aged walls, were keenly aware of the superb edifice and its historic significance. They successfully fought Governor Huey Long's plan to raze the building and replace it with a rose garden. The Manchac chapter of the Daughters of the American Revolution was also successful in rescuing the arsenal from destruction in 1955, when plans were being drafted to build the state library on its site.

The cause of historic preservation was truly served in July 1962 when the Old Arsenal Museum was officially opened to the citizens of our state and nation. Appropriately using the theme "Louisiana Under Ten Flags," this museum was used to house exhibits depicting the many phases of Louisiana's colorful heritage. It draws the global strings tighter since it indelibly binds our past not just with that of our nation but also with that of Europe. These walls, which once witnessed nervous young lieutenants supervising the storage of deadly explosives, now host countless visitors annually from all over the world who come to catch a glimpse of Louisiana's historic treasures and military history.

Old Arsenal Museum, aerial view. *Photo by Layne Photography.*

On June 4, 1973, the Old Arsenal Museum was placed on the National Register of Historic Places. Unfortunately, the exhibits shown under the "Louisiana Under Ten Flags" theme were closed sometime between 1986 and 1988. Gone are the glass-encased life-sized figures of Hernando de Soto and Pierre Le Moyne Sieur d'Iberville, among others, dressed in period costumes. At present, the museum contains displays about the structure of this historic powder magazine.

PENTAGON BARRACKS

The massive salmon-colored buildings jut into the skyline on a high bluff overlooking the Mississippi River as if defiantly announcing their declaration of permanence. The breezes that waft upward from the river and across the former parade grounds reiterate this claim for its perpetuity. These buildings compose Louisiana's famed Pentagon Barracks. While Washington, D.C., can claim the largest Pentagon Barracks in the United States, they were not built until 1941. Baton Rouge's Pentagon Barracks, completed by 1822, can easily claim to be the oldest. As such, these buildings cry out to be maintained, not only as memorials to the famous and ordinary men who served and

Pentagon Barracks, aerial view. *Courtesy of the Louisiana Office of Tourism.*

visited here but also as historic shrines for the many great statesmen and soldiers who have lived and worked here, as well as for the present and future edification of our citizens.

Rising more than sixteen feet above the Mississippi River, the plot of ground on which the two-storied Greek Doric buildings stand is a historic site. In 1779, the British erected a dirt fort on the site. With the outbreak of the Revolutionary War in 1776, the fort later became a threat to the forthcoming new republic and its ally, Spain. The barracks were then captured by the Spanish governor of Louisiana, Bernardo de Gálvez (see map on page 10). The fear of being defeated in battle and subjected to Spanish rule forced the citizens of the West Florida Territory in 1810 to revolt, declare their independence and announce the birth of the Republic of West Florida. Under their president, Fulwar Skipwith, the citizens then turned over the territory to the United States in December 1810. Thus, this territory has the distinction of being the site of the birth of a short-lived nation, the Republic of West Florida. It has also served as a battleground for the armies of France, Spain, England and the United States in the struggle for supremacy of the Mississippi River Valley. Eight different flags have flown over this bluff, more than for any other capital city. It has been won and lost by the Spanish, French and the British. During this period, this fort served as the base for American troops going to the Creek Wars from 1813 to 1814 and to the Battle of New Orleans from 1814 to 1815.

But what about the long-galleried, pillared buildings that now rest sedately on this legendary ground? As part of a master plan to build a system of interior fortification, the United States government purchased these lands belonging to Fergus Duplantier for $13,500 on May 27, 1819, to begin a military post in Baton Rouge. The relics of the old Spanish Fort San Carlos, which had replaced the British fort, were razed to clear the ground. There are varying accounts of when construction of the buildings began and fascinating tales of the problems encountered, even and including a yellow fever epidemic. What is known for certain is that in 1819 Captain James Gadsen, United States Army engineer, drafted a plan for a pentagonal group of buildings and a nearby powder magazine. The barracks consisted of four two-storied buildings, allowing an open space on the fifth side of the pentagon. The four structures were and are still lettered counterclockwise, with Building A on the southwest, Building B on the southeast, Building C on the northeast and Building D on the north.

All four buildings were constructed of brick, with ten large Doric pillars that supported the two-story galleries on the front and rear of each one. Buildings A and D are 184 feet long and 34 feet wide, with two galleries that are each 12 feet wide. Buildings B and C are each 24 feet wide, plus the two galleries, which are 12 feet each. The upper floors of four of the buildings were to be used as barracks for a regiment of troops and as quarters for the officers on the post. The ground floors were designed for use as kitchens, mess halls, storerooms, offices and guardhouse. The fifth building consisted of two identical buildings, end to end—twin structures with a common wall. It was to be used by the Quartermaster and the Commissary Departments.

John Hill, who had been hired as the contractor, imported brick makers, brick masons and carpenters from Ohio, Kentucky and New England. They started construction in June 1819. By September 1819, a yellow fever epidemic had taken the lives of thirty artisans and twenty soldiers. Despite this, all the annals concur that most of the work on the barracks was completed in 1822 after Zachary Taylor assumed command of the First U.S. Infantry Regiment post here. The fort remained a U.S. military post until 1861, when it was captured by Louisiana troops, and then it was recaptured by Federal troops in 1862 after the Battle of Baton Rouge.

These brick army barracks have defied conventional description since the beginning. To start with, they were named the Pentagon Barracks. A dictionary defines a pentagon as having five sides, but Louisiana's pentagonal group today only has four buildings, or four sides. Innumerable stories have circulated about this alleged "misnomer." They range from a flat denial of the existence of a fifth building to descriptions of how this building was destroyed by fire, tidal wave or a cyclone. During the Civil War in 1862, however, Federal troops reclaimed the garrison and renamed it Fort Williams. In 1870, an official United States Army report that was filed following the capture of the garrison should have ended the speculation. It clearly notes that the fifth building, located on the bank and parallel to the Mississippi River, was removed. Thus, in recording its removal, this report gives a logical claim to the existence of the fifth building. It also lends credence to earlier accounts that the fifth barrack was removed because of its inferior workmanship.

The other four barracks were so well built that they have survived to the present day despite their proximity to the Mississippi River and vulnerability

Pentagon Barracks, front view. *Courtesy of the Louisiana Office of Tourism.*

to numerous Category 5 hurricanes. The buildings are endowed with broad galleries, both in the front and in the rear, supported by imposing brick columns. Until 1877, the ground floors of these pentagons were used as classrooms, while the second floors provided living quarters for the cadets. Except for the brief interlude when the fort was held by the Confederacy, countless cadets and every important United States Army officer during this fifty-five-year span, from 1822 to 1877, were either trained or stationed here at some point in their military careers. The names of Robert E. Lee, Ulysses Grant, William Tecumseh Sherman and P.G.T. Beauregard, among others, are inscribed in the rolls. Some of the famous individuals who visited the Pentagon Barracks include Abraham Lincoln, Jefferson Davis, John C. Calhoun, James K. Polk, Thomas Jonathon "Stonewall" Jackson, Henry Clay, Winfield Scott, George Armstrong Custer and Gilbert du Motier, the Marquis de Lafayette.

After 1877, the barracks were abandoned as an army post. For nine years, the buildings and the parade grounds were muted to all sounds except those surfacing from the past. Perhaps old memories of French and Spanish soldiers blended with those of American frontiersmen,

Pentagon Barracks, close-up of front gallery. *Courtesy of the Louisiana Office of Tourism.*

adventurers and secessionists. During this period, some visitors claimed that they heard marching footsteps on the parade grounds and the distant sound of galloping hoof beats. The latter, an old guide claimed, simulated those first made by Jefferson Davis's horse on the day he rode onto the parade ground to elope with Zachary Taylor's daughter. Romance, mystery and intrigue had already wrapped these buildings and grounds in a protective shield.

Fortunately, the discarded Pentagon became Louisiana State University's official home in 1886. It was on special loan from the federal government, thanks to the efforts of William Tecumseh Sherman and David French Boyd. By 1927, the university cadets were quartered in the buildings at the new campus. The coeds also moved into the barracks that same year. In their honor, the buildings had been completely remodeled at a cost of $50,000. Instead of with the sounds made by marching cadets, the parade grounds now rumbled with the clicking of high heels and music blaring from phonographs. Within five years, even these sounds were silenced when Louisiana State University discontinued use of the renovated barracks as dormitories.

According to an old newspaper account, the barracks were then slowly converted into a series of forty-four modern apartments that came to be known as the Pentagon Court. The university rented these mainly to its faculty and staff members.

In 1951, the Louisiana State University Board of Supervisors voted to transfer its Pentagon Barracks to the state. The legislature quickly passed a law sanctioning this transfer, and thus the last tie was severed between present-day Louisiana State University and the "Ole War Skule" of past years. By legislative decree, three of the buildings were converted into offices to house state agencies, and the fourth was reserved to become apartments for state officials.

Today, the fate of these venerable walls has once again been altered by legislative act. This time, all the state agencies housed in the historic buildings are being moved as quickly as possible and relocated to far-flung sections of Baton Rouge, for the legislature has decreed that all the buildings be vacated in order to convert them into apartments for the legislature. The parade ground has now become a battleground between the legislature and civic groups intent on preserving these four barracks as a national shrine. Presently, the Pentagon Barracks house the offices of the lieutenant governor and private apartments for state legislators.

CURTISS P-40 WARHAWK, "JOY"

Close to the USS *Kidd* at the riverside war memorial, there is a vintage Curtiss P-40 Warhawk airplane named "Joy." It is one of the remaining vestiges of the legendary "Flying Tigers" fighting air force. It is painted in the original colors of this group and marked with the tiger shark's face. As one of the airplanes in the First American Volunteer Group of the Chinese air force, it first saw combat in December 1941, twelve days after Pearl Harbor was attacked by surprise. Formally incorporated into the United States Army Air Forces in 1942, this group of airmen, which was composed of international volunteers, made innovative tactical and daring contributions to the aerial attacks against the Japanese. The international air force, called the American Volunteer Group, led by Major General Claire Lee Chennault, commander of the Fourteenth Air Force in China, developed into a crack fighting unit. Always fighting superior Japanese forces and usually victorious at a time when the news was filled with little more than stories of defeat at the hands of the Japanese, they became the symbol of United States' military strength in Asia.

This airplane was once a part of three fighter squadrons with about twenty aircraft each. Claire L. Chennault had spent part of the winter of 1940–41 in Washington, D.C., supervising the purchase of one hundred Curtiss P-40 fighter planes through the Office of China Defense Supplies. Money for this purchase was loaned surreptitiously by the government of the United States. These planes had been diverted from an original British Royal Air Force order that had been canceled by the British when they thought the Curtiss P-40 planes were obsolete.

The Curtiss P-40 Warhawk came from a Curtiss factory assembly line in North Africa producing the Tomahawk IIB model for the Royal Air Force. Similar to the United States Army's earlier P-40B model, there is some evidence that Curtiss used some of its parts for the model used to build the fighter planes destined for China. Unfortunately, these were built without reflector gun sights, radios and wing guns, which caused major problems for future pilots. The P-40 fighter planes in this group were painted with large shark faces on the fronts of the aircraft. Because of Chennault's association with Louisiana State University, alumni of this university fantasized that he had named his famous flying corps after its "Fighting Tigers" football team. In reality, Chennault supposedly named his corps in deference to the Chinese reverence for the sleek, ruthless tiger shark. A second piece of information is that the fighter aircraft was painted with the large shark face

Claire Chennault statue beside the plane. *Photo by Layne Photography.*

on the front after some of the pilots saw a photograph of a P-40 of the Luftwaffe's 112 Squadron Royal Air Force in North Africa. They, in turn, had adopted the shark face from German pilots of the ZG 76 heavy fighter wing, flying Messerschmitt BF 110 fighters in Crete.

Major General Chennault, the organizer of this squadron, began his career in the United States Army Air Corps during World War I when he earned his first lieutenant's commission. Even then, the stern, no-nonsense Chennault was considered a controversial aviator because he supported General Billy Mitchell and his revolutionary air fighting tactics. Following this inclination, he enrolled and graduated from pursuit pilot training at Ellington Field, Texas, in 1922. By the 1930s, he had become the chief of the pursuit section of the Air Corps Tactical School. With this specialized training and a contentious advocate of "pursuit" (or fight interceptor) aircraft, he was confident that he could train his pilots to fly the P-40s successfully against the superior Japanese planes.

The training of pilots and fighter planes began in Burma prior to the entry of the United States into World War II. Chennault had studied Japanese flying tactics and equipment. He had also studied the techniques employed by the Russian units while serving with the Chinese air force. Armed with this information and his judgment of the strengths and weaknesses of his own airplanes and pilots, he created a formidable fighting force. He instructed his pilots to form in groups and engage the enemy aircraft from an altitude advantage, and he ordered them never to engage in a turning fight with the more maneuverable Japanese fighter planes but rather to perform diving or slashing attacks and then dive again to set up another attack. Spurred on by Chennault's brilliant leadership and revolutionary air tactics, these pilots flew their planes in such a manner that they overcame their inferior numbers and equipment. Also aided by the Chinese warning network system, the air fighter group could fully utilize the advantages of its air tactics and was able to claim innumerable victories with legendary feats of courage and boldness.

While fighting to protect China and the Burma Road against the oppressive forces of Japan and its allies, the "Flying Tigers," flying their Curtis P-40s, became the only Allied force that won any victories in the early days of World War II against the mighty Axis forces of Germany, Italy and Japan. It's no wonder that when English Prime Minister Winston Churchill met Chennault at the Cairo Conference, he said, "I'm glad he's on our side."

The actual strength of the "Flying Tigers" never exceeded more than fifty-five flyable P-40s, 80 pilots and 132 mechanics in their ready-to-fight task force. Motivated by salaries three times higher than the average salary in the United States forces, plus a verbal promise of a $500 bounty for each enemy plane shot down, this daredevil group of pilots was exceptionally inspired to achieve daring feats. During the time that Hitler's Luftwaffe was sweeping across European skies, gaining air dominance and bombing London to rubble, General Chennault's "Flying Tigers" inspired the Allies by soundly defeating overwhelming Japanese air forces and smashing Japanese shipping along China's coast. This American volunteer group easily became the most famous fighting group to surface from World War II.

It is impossible to view the Curtiss P-40 Warhawk "Joy," parked at the riverside war memorial, without remembering the son of Louisiana who gave this plane its prominence. The plane admittedly had some serious defects that made its use questionable. But because of Lieutenant General Claire Lee Chennault's military genius and dogged determination, he turned it into a victorious instrument for peace. His statue, which once appropriately stood by this P-40, is no longer there. The bronze statute had also once stood tall on its magnificent marble pedestal overlooking the grounds at the Pentagon Barracks across from Louisiana's New State Capitol Building. It had been presented by Nationalist China to the State of Louisiana as an expression of gratitude for Chennault's invaluable help against the Japanese and the forces of Communism. On the crisp October day in 1976 when the statue was unveiled, the second wife and Chinese-born widow of the air ace and hero, in the presence of then Governor Edwin Edwards and several former "Flying Tigers," told the crowd that her husband would be "proud and honored that we all remember."

MEMORIAL TOWER, OR CAMPANILE, AT LOUISIANA STATE UNIVERSITY

Like a glittering jewel in the crown that perches atop the Baton Rouge campus of Louisiana State University, the Memorial Tower—or Campanile, as it is interchangeably called—rises 175 feet tall, as if surveying all the buildings and activities within the scope of its view. This encompasses quite a great deal, for this university campus is the flagship institution for the Louisiana State University System. As such, it is one of only thirty universities in the nation holding land-grant, sea-grant and space-grant status. When Chancellor Mark Emmert led the creation of the flagship agenda, with its focus centered on augmenting student quality and research productivity, it catapulted LSU into the enviable position of being regarded as one of the finest public universities in the nation. This Memorial Tower is in the heart of the campus, and some say that it is the heart of the institution.

Built in the early 1920s, the clock tower was dedicated in 1926 as a memorial to Louisianans who died in World War I. It remains the anchor in the cruciform quadrangle around which the original architects centered their campus design and gives a purpose to the plaza area directly in its front view. It also serves the specific purpose of all clock towers, which is to keep the students and faculty constantly in touch with the time and their daily schedules. As an added bonus, this Memorial Tower adds considerable beauty to the landscape of the campus.

The Memorial Tower was one of the first buildings completed on the LSU campus. The original architectural firm, Olmsted Brothers of Massachusetts, designed the general outlay of the current campus in about 1921. It had envisioned that the buildings at LSU would be charted with a Spanish-style motif. Without any explanation whatsoever, this firm was dismissed in favor of an architect by the name of Theodore Link. Perhaps his selection as the architect reflected the fact that his architectural blueprint was more akin to Huey P. Long's desire that the tower be built to resemble the historic clock tower at the basilica in Vicenza, Italy. Link's blueprint was in keeping with the architectural movement pervading at the time that reflected an eclectic style with its roots in the French Beaux Arts system.

LSU Memorial Tower as seen from the parade grounds. *Photo by Layne Photography.*

Whatever the case may have been, while incorporating Olmsted's overall basic plan for the university, the new architect designed the campus with red-tiled roofs, tan stucco walls and extensive porticos. The design emulated the architecture of Italian Renaissance architect Andrea Palladio, who incidentally had designed the clock tower in Vicenza, Italy. Thus, it is no surprise that the Memorial Tower is fashioned in the traditional Italian Renaissance style of architecture called the campanile, which means "bell tower" in Italian. (The most famous example of this artistic design is the Leaning Tower of Pisa.) Link had the misfortune to die in 1923 before his plan was completed. New Orleans architects Wogan and Bernard took over Link's work and finished the Memorial Tower. The American Legion, having conducted a statewide drive for this express purpose, had collected the funds to pay for the tower and then presented a check to the university to cover the costs.

The cornerstone in front of the tower was excavated from the ruins of Louisiana State Seminary of Learning and Military Academy in Pineville, an earlier version of LSU. This foundation stone describes the history of LSU on one side and is inscribed with the names of the members of the first board of supervisors on the other side. The entrance to the tower features a lobby and, above it, an arched ceiling. The rotunda inside the tower has bronze plaques on the walls bearing the names of the 1,447 fallen Louisiana soldiers to whom the tower is dedicated. At different times, the rotunda has also served as an exhibition facility for different collections, including the permanent collection of the LSU Museum of Art. A narrow metal staircase winds its way along the inside of the tower walls and ends at a room where the actual clockwork is housed. Above the clockwork and high above the campus, there is a viewing area with wide arches. Although the arches are covered with chicken wire to prevent birds from roosting inside, they still allow visitors to partake of a spectacular view. The original "bells" that used to ring from the tower were once located in this viewing area. For the Memorial Tower, the "bells" themselves were never traditional bells like the Liberty Bell; thus, perhaps it could more accurately be called a "chime tower" rather than a "bell tower."

It goes without saying that the express purpose for clock towers is their timepiece, which includes the clock itself linked to the chimes or bells. This type of clock is known as a striking clock, and its mechanism inside the tower is known as a turret clock. In the fifteenth century, the size of the clocks and what encased them increased, making it possible to house the mechanism that could strike a large bell with the possibility of hitting a number of bells or chimes corresponding to the hour or hours that were to be indicated. To increase the audible range of the chimes or bells, the clocks were mounted in a tower, and thus the clock tower was born. A typical striking clock would have two gear trains, one timekeeping train that would measure the passage of time and another gear called a striking train, which would operate the mechanism that rings the bell or chimes.

The first clock used in the Memorial Tower was probably manufactured by the Seth Thomas Clock Company from Thomaston, Connecticut, considered to be one of the premier clock manufacturers in the United States. The face of the clock in the Memorial Tower presents, and has always presented, a rather unusual characteristic: it displays the fourth numeral as "IIII" rather than the usual Roman numeral denoted as

"IV." Historically, clock towers did not have faces or dials until the late eighteenth century, and it is possible that the designers lacked the necessary years of experience in developing the outside faces of the clocks. (In time, clock tower designers realized that placing a dial on the outside of the tower would allow the townspeople to check the time whenever they so desired and thus doubly serve the purpose for which they were designed in that they could see the time and hear the chimes.) This deviation in the numerals, however, is rather commonplace among clock towers. According to Logan Leger in the *Baton Rougean* in 2009, there are many theories concerning why this oddity occurred, some "lost in hundreds of years of tradition." Perhaps the best proposed theory or explanation lies in the fact that, aesthetically, the manner in which the fourth numeral is displayed seems to be the most pleasing to the eye. There is balance and symmetry in the face of this clock tower.

The first chimes used in the tower were bought with funds donated by Colonel Edward G. Schlieder of New Orleans in 1925. Originally, they were eighteen tube chimes, not bells. These chimes spanned about an octave and a half, and were listed in a catalogue of the 1930s. This same catalogue valued a set of such "bells" at $10,000, with the total set weighing almost five tons. The original chimes were replaced with automated chimes in 1949. By 1960, the automated chimes had been replaced by a new roll-type carillon by J.C. Deagan. They were the Deagan chimes, a series of straight, vertical hanging bells. When the carillon was replaced in 1979, these chimes mysteriously vanished, and no one seems to know what happened to them. They were replaced by a tape and loudspeaker system made by I.T. Verdin Company, preeminent manufacturer in the United States of Verdin Bells and Clocks for more than 170 years.

Twenty-seven years later, between 2006 and 2007, compliments of the LSU student government, the tape and loudspeaker system in turn were replaced by an electronic recording, which is run by a computer. Mr. Michael Guillory, director of Facility Systems, stated that the speakers play a recording of the actual Deagan chimes. He added that "[w]e had to do some research on what the real LSU bell sound was. We had all kinds of people try to tell us what that sound was, but in the end we came up with a great representation." This new system is programmable and operated by a computer on the tower's ground floor.

Today, the "bells" are actually a series of huge speakers that sit atop the tower, high above the university and accessible only by a ladder that climbs up a story from the viewing area. Pointing in every direction, they resemble oversized megaphones and are capable of a large repertoire. There is even a keyboard that can be hooked up to allow a musician to "play" the chimes. Except at noon, LSU's melodious chimes ring every quarter hour until 10:00 p.m., playing the Westminster Quarters. At noon, however, the bells play the university's alma mater loud and clear. On the days when LSU plays football, the chimes at noon play the LSU march song, recorded by the LSU Golden Band from Tiger Land, intended to muster and arouse school spirit. At that time, that song supplants everything as the most distinguished and important refrain on the campus. But there are very few deviations from the norm, for the chancellor's office must give official approval before any changes can be made to the bells' schedule. To the best of our knowledge, the last time the schedule varied occurred when it played hymns for a candlelight vigil in honor of the victims of the 2007 Virginia Tech shooting. Everyone in Baton Rouge wants to preserve the mystique of the tower and not change anything about it on a whim. This is another example of mankind trying to hang on to its known past.

There is an interesting and important tradition regarding the ringing of the chimes, and it can be a romantic aside. This one claims that a student must be kissed underneath the tower when the chimes ring at midnight in order to become an "official LSU student." Needless to say, Valentine's Day is the only day the campanile rings after 10:00 p.m. On February 14, then, it doesn't matter that the clock face deviates from the normal with its unusual rendition of the Roman numeral four. When those chimes ring, every LSU student and alumni within hearing range feels a special tug at the heartstrings.

The Memorial Tower has other traditions that keep it in the center of campus life. The plaza in front of it also hosts events annually that keep it in the limelight. The induction of the new president and vice-president of the Student Government Association takes place in front of the tower every spring. A number of military and other appropriate university ceremonies are held there throughout the year. "Free Speech Alley" draws a large audience. The annual lighting of the university's Christmas tree, which decorates the campus for the holiday season, is another event that attracts students, visitors and people from the Baton Rouge community to the campus. In summary, the Memorial Tower is not only the focal point of LSU, but it also represents a large piece of the capital city of Louisiana.

USS *KIDD* (DD-661)

It is difficult to write about a monument that happens to be a legendary destroyer. We can praise the beauty of its sleek lines, the resilient strength and power of its engines and the exceptional firing power of its varied guns, but where can we describe the magnitude of the emotions that followed it throughout the different theaters of war all over the world? Along with the trail of broken hearts left on sea and land, where are the joyous "hellos" and gut-wrenching "goodbyes" recorded? We suspect that they are chronicled somewhere on the decks and bulkheads of the mighty ship we know as the USS *Kidd.* While the memories left of the abomination that is war are difficult to document, we can write about how it came into being, attempt to describe the long and varied history of its naval career and narrate details about its final resting place.

The USS *Kidd* (DD-661) is permanently moored on the Mississippi River in downtown Baton Rouge. It is one of only four Fletcher-design destroyers built by the United States during World War II that has been preserved for posterity in the world today. It is also the first United States Navy ship to be named for Rear Admiral Isaac C. Kidd, who was killed on the bridge of his flagship the USS *Arizona* during the Japanese sneak attack on Pearl Harbor on December 7,

USS *Kidd* (DD-661). *Photo by Layne Photography.*

1941—a day President Roosevelt stated will live in infamy in the annals of the history of war and of our nation. Rear Admiral Kidd was the first U.S. Navy flag officer to be killed during World War II and was also the first naval officer to meet death while in action against any foreign enemy. He was the recipient of the Medal of Honor and a Purple Heart. So deservedly christened to honor Kidd's name, this destroyer was aesthetically reinstated to late–World War II configuration and recognized by the Historic Naval Ships Association as one of the most authentically restored vessels across five continents. It has a long and glorious history of defending the safety and integrity of the United States. Baton Rouge is proud and honored to be its final resting place.

The Fletcher-style destroyer was designed in 1939, and its innovative aspects revealed military dissatisfaction with the earlier destroyer-leader types. The 2,100 tonners were significantly larger than any of the other previous American destroyer classes. They had a design speed of thirty-eight knots, were armed with five five-inch guns in single mounts and carried ten twenty-one-inch torpedoes in twin quintuple centerline mounts. Between 1942 and 1944, the United States Navy commissioned 175 of the Fletcher-class destroyers, a significantly larger amount than any other class of destroyer. These long-range Fletcher-class ships could participate in every aspect of battle that was required of them. They could engage in antisubmarine warfare, antiaircraft conflict or surface combat.

Because they were the first large ships of their type to appear in naval battles, and because there were so many of them, the Fletcher-style ships are remembered as the signature U.S. Navy destroyer of their class in the Pacific Theater of operations during World War II. During this time, and among other statistics, they accounted for the sinking of twenty-nine Japanese imperial navy submarines. The first ones launched battled during the nighttime surface skirmishes in the Solomon Islands. Many of them saw action at Leyte in the Philippines, and all of them participated in screenings of enemy ships for the fleet, shore bombardment assignments and the renowned anti-kamikaze radar picket duty at Okinawa. Unfortunately, nineteen of these ships were lost and six damaged beyond repair. However, the remaining forty-four Fletcher-type destroyers earned ten or more service stars each, while nineteen of them were awarded the Navy Unit Commendation. Sixteen of them were honorably singled out to receive the Presidential Unit Citation.

The particular Fletcher-class destroyer that is anchored here (the USS *Kidd*) was built by Federal Shipbuilding & Drydock Company in Kearny, New Jersey. It was launched on February 28, 1943, and sponsored by Mrs. Isaac C. Kidd, Rear Admiral Kidd's widow. The USS *Kidd* was commissioned on April 23, 1943, with Commander Allan Roby at the helm. Its initial cruise was to the Brooklyn Naval Shipyards, sailing across New York Harbor with the "Jolly Roger" on the foremast. Since the black flag with the white skull and crossbones was the emblem of piracy, the crew subsequently adopted the pirate captain William Kidd as their mascot. The crew went so far as to commission a local artist to decorate the forward smokestack with a painting of the figure of a pirate.

In June 1943, after leaving Casco Bay, Maine, the *Kidd* cruised in the Atlantic Ocean and the Caribbean Sea as the escort for large combatant vessels. Along with the USS *Alabama* and the USS *South Dakota*, it departed for the Pacific Ocean in August 1943 and arrived at Pearl Harbor on September 17, 1943. By September 29, the *Kidd* was escorting aircraft carriers toward Wake Island to help deliver the heavy air attacks there on October 6. It returned to Pearl Harbor on October 11, 1943, and by mid-October it was accompanying a task force to strike the heavily fortified Japanese island of Rabaul and support the troop landings on the nearby island of Bougainville. Reaching a striking position south of Rabaul by November 11, the American task force attacked the Japanese positions on the island. The USS *Essex*, a part of the task force, lost an aircraft during the attack when it crashed behind the formation. The *Kidd* was ordered to go into the thick of battle to rescue the surviving members of the crew floating in the water. Again, we can only imagine the horror and magnitude of the cannons firing, the bombs exploding and the torpedoes launching all occurring during the rescue attempts. While it was fulfilling this command, Japanese aircraft also attacked the destroyer. Heroically, the *Kidd* shot down three of the attacking aircraft and completed the rescue while still maneuvering to dodge the torpedoes, gunfire and bombs. Commander Alan Roby, officer in charge, received the Silver Star for exceptional bravery and gallantry during this battle.

November 13, 1943, saw the destroyer sail southeast to Espiritu Santo. While there, from the nineteenth to the twenty-third of November during the American invasion of the Gilbert Islands, the *Kidd* was serving as a screen for the aircraft carriers that were delivering air attacks on Tarawa. On November 24, spotting fifteen low-flying enemy bombers heading for the heavy ships in its task force, it alerted those in command about the forthcoming arrival of the aircraft. During this time, it also shot down two "Val" dive bombers. After helping to secure Tarawa, the *Kidd* remained in the Gilbert Islands, assisting with the clean-up operations before returning to Pearl Harbor on December 9, 1943. It belonged to the group of Fletcher-class destroyers that almost exclusively served in the Pacific Theater during World War II, during which time this group accounted for the sinking of twenty-nine Japanese imperial navy submarines.

On January 11, 1944, the *Kidd* sailed for Espiritu Santo again. Once there, it sailed on the following day to Funafuti, arriving there on January 19. It began island-hopping on the atolls of the Pacific Ocean, the steppingstones to reach the mainland of Japan. The invasion of the Marshall Islands took place from January 29 to February 8, and during this time, the Fletcher-style destroyer screened the heavy Japanese ships and kept the other members of the American task force informed of their whereabouts. It bombarded Roi and Wotje and then anchored on one of the islands on the Kwajalein Atoll on February 26. From March 20 to April 14, the *Kidd* guarded an airstrip that was under construction on the island of Emirau from air attacks and subsequently helped support the occupation of Aitape and Hollandia in New Guinea from April 17 to May 7. Between June 10 and July 8, it fought in the Marianas Campaign, followed by shore bombardment duty in Guam between July 8 and August 10.

Badly in need of repairs and servicing, the *Kidd* sailed for Pearl Harbor, arriving on August 26, 1944. In about three weeks, it was able to depart Pearl Harbor, reaching the island of Eniwetok on September 26 and arriving at Manus on October 3. There, it became a part of the giant American Philippines invasion fleet and entered Leyte Gulf on October 20. Once again, it assisted in providing a screen for the initial landings and furnished invaluable fire support for the American soldiers invading and fighting to conquer the Japanese-held island of Mindanao, the southernmost island in the Philippines. On November 14, it sailed for Humboldt Bay, New Guinea, and arrived there on November 19. By December 9, the *Kidd* was heading for Mare Island Navy Yard, north of San Francisco Bay, for an overhaul, arriving there on Christmas Day 1944.

Preparing to assist with the invasion of Okinawa, the destroyer sailed on February 19, 1945, and joined Task Force 58 (TF 58). Trained and experienced in combat, it played a major role during the battle for Iwo Jima, a battle that has been described as one in which men met their deaths in the most violent, bloody manner possible. Then it sailed slightly northwest to participate in the first days of the Okinawa Campaign. The *Kidd* multitasked by providing screens for the larger battleships, bombarding shore targets, providing early warning of raids, sinking floating mines and guarding and protecting the heavily damaged USS *Franklin* (CV-13). During all this time, it was shooting down Japanese kamikaze planes and rescuing downed pilots from the seas.

While on picket station on April 11, 1945, the *Kidd* and its division mates, USS *Black*, USS *Bullard* and USS *Chauncey*, assisted by Combat Air Patrol, were able to repel three air raids. Picket station duty was particularly onerous and sacrificial, for it required the Fletcher-style destroyers to form a picket line a certain distance from their task force and surround the larger ships and aircraft carriers in their task force. They were also to provide a radar screen, warning the other members of their group about the proximity of approaching enemy aircraft. The young, inexperienced Japanese pilots mistook the destroyers on the picket line as their main targets and acted accordingly. Fortunately, these Japanese pilots missed most of their targets. Unfortunately, one afternoon in April, a single Japanese kamikaze plane crashed into the *Kidd*, killing thirty-eight men and wounding fifty-five. As the *Kidd* headed south attempting to rejoin its task force, the raging fire on the deck caused by the kamikaze attack repelled the enemy planes trying to finish it off and sink it. It was able to sail on and stop at Ulithi for temporary repairs.

After leaving Ulithi, the *Kidd* headed for the West Coast of the United States on May 2 and arrived at Hunter's Point Naval Shipyard on May 25. On August 1, 1945, it sailed to Pearl Harbor and then on to San Diego, California, in September 1945 to be deactivated. It was decommissioned on December 10, 1946, and became a member of the Pacific Reserve Fleet. It had participated in the heavy action in World War II in the Pacific Ocean. It had fought with unsurpassed skill and bravery during the invasions of the Gilbert Islands and the Marshall Islands; the invasion of the Philippines at Leyte Gulf; and, finally, the invasion of Okinawa, where the battles that took place were even fiercer than the ones it had experienced on Iwo Jima. The *Kidd* had indeed earned more than its keep.

But the *Kidd* was not finished serving its country yet. When North Korea attacked South Korea on June 28, 1950, crossing the thirty-eighth parallel, the United States was obliged to call up a portion of the reserve fleet. As part of that call, the *Kidd* was recommissioned on March 28, 1951, with Lieutenant Commander Robert E. Jeffery in command. It sailed to the western Pacific Ocean on June 18, arriving at Yokosuka, Japan, on July 15. There it joined Task Force 77 and served on patrol off the western Korean coast until September, followed by an assignment to the eastern coast of Korea. From October 21, 1951, to January 22, 1952, it bombarded targets in that area from Wan-Do Island to below Koesong. When its mission was completed, the destroyer sailed with Destroyer Division 152 to San Diego, California, and reached there on February 6, 1952.

The *Kidd* got underway again on September 8, 1952, and headed for Korea to join in the screen of a hunter-killer group near Kojo. By November, it was bombarding targets off the coast of North Korea. When the truce talks began, the destroyer continued to patrol the Korean coast during the negotiations. By March 3, 1953, it had left the Far East via Pearl Harbor and arrived in San Diego, California, for an overhaul on March 20 of the same year.

After the overhaul of the ship was completed and the Korean War was over, the Fletcher-style destroyer left for Long Beach, California, on April 20, 1953. The day after it got there, the Swedish freighter *Hainan* collided with it in the harbor, requiring repairs that lasted until May 11, 1953. Later in 1953 and until 1959, the *Kidd* took turns making cruises in the West Pacific while participating in naval operations on the West Coast. During this time, stops were made at Pearl Harbor and different ports in Japan, Okinawa, Hong Kong and the Philippines. The destroyer also visited Sydney, Australia, on March 29, 1958, and patrolled the Taiwan Strait later in the year.

In January 1960, the *Kidd* sailed for the East Coast via the Panama Canal, arriving in Philadelphia later that month. From Philadelphia, it participated in Naval Reserve training cruises to various ports along the East Coast. During the Berlin crisis in 1961, it was a member of the fleet operating forces. Also in December of that year, it was on patrol off the coast of the Dominican Republic, mainly as a show of force to provide some security in the unsettled waters of the Caribbean. In early 1962, it arrived in Norfolk, Virginia, to join Task Force Alpha for exercises in antisubmarine warfare. By April, it had been assigned to the Naval Destroyer School at Newport, Rhode Island. Following a cruise to the Caribbean in July 1962, it resumed Naval Reserve training for close to two years until it was decommissioned on June 19, 1964, entered the Atlantic Reserve Fleet and berthed at the Philadelphia Shipyard.

There are four Fletcher-class destroyers that have been preserved in the world for public display. There is one in Greece, the former *Charrette*, renamed the *Velos*, which remains a popular attraction. In the 1980s, the United States Navy reserved three Fletcher-class destroyers to be used as memorials in the United States: the USS *Sullivans* (DD-537), docked in Buffalo; the USS *Cassin Young* (DD-793), harbored in Boston; and the USS *Kidd* (DD-661), moored in Baton Rouge, Louisiana. Congressman William Henson Moore selected the *Kidd* to serve as a memorial for Louisiana's World War II veterans. Accordingly, it was towed from Philadelphia and arrived in Baton Rouge on May 23, 1982, where it was immediately transferred to the authority and ownership of the Louisiana Naval War Commission.

As we view the USS *Kidd* today in Baton Rouge, resting in its one-of-a-kind docking cradle that allows it to stay afloat six months of the year

USS *Kidd*, as seen on the Fourth of July. *Courtesy of Wilbur Rogers and Art Colley.*

and then be in dry-dock the remainder of the year, we all sit in wonder and amazement at its valiant and storied past. Participating in the bloodiest and most horrific naval battles in the Pacific Ocean during World War II and later in Korea, it even managed to survive a deadly Japanese kamikaze attack. It took on the best and strongest that the Axis powers had available to throw at it and defeated them. It is no wonder that the *Kidd* earned the eight battle stars it received for its services to the country in World War II and the four additional battle stars accorded for its Korean War service. Its name is on the National Register of Historic Places, and it is a National Historic Landmark.

It is still in service to its country even today. Where once it was home to three hundred sailors at a time during their tour of duty, today it serves as a base to honor veterans of all wars and all branches of service; to educate children and adults about ships and naval affairs; and to host youth groups in overnight camping programs. However, on the Fourth of July every year, the USS *Kidd* resumes active duty. In fact, it has fought the Independence Day battle from the Mississippi River for more years than it served on active duty in the navy. For the last twenty-three years, the veteran destroyer has taken on "fighting" vintage Japanese aircraft in such realistically staged "battles" that the public gets a good picture of what World War II–era combat was like. The guns on the

Kidd, though, fire only a one-pound powder charge rather than the customary seventeen-pound charge, for fear of shattering the windows on the buildings in downtown Baton Rouge. During the reenactments of these "battles," we wonder if the *Kidd*'s bulkheads reverberate with the echoes and human sounds of past battles, both won and lost.

CIVIL WAR BRASS CANNONS AT LSU's AEROSPACE STUDIES AND MILITARY SCIENCE BUILDING

Guarding the entrance of the Aerospace Studies and Military Science Building at Louisiana State University's Baton Rouge campus are two brass fourteen-pounder James Rifle cannons that saw action at Fort Sumter during the Civil War, starting in 1861. They serve as present-day reminders of the university's past and its connection to a seminary of learning and military academy and harbor the memory of a certain General William Tecumseh Sherman.

The presence of cannons on a university campus, particularly in front of a military science building, is not that surprising given that three of LSU's presidents have been well-known and respected military generals. The first

Brass cannons at the LSU Aerospace Studies and Military Science Building. *Photo by Layne Photography.*

of these presidents was William Tecumseh Sherman, who in 1859 accepted the job of being the first superintendent of the Louisiana State Seminary of Learning and Military Academy, which was created in 1853 by the Louisiana General Assembly. He was reportedly an effective and popular leader until 1861, when the outbreak of the Civil War and Louisiana's subsequent secession from the Union forced him to resign. In his letter of resignation to Louisiana Governor Thomas O. Moore, Sherman stated, "I prefer to maintain allegiance to the Constitution as long as a fragment of it survives." With the onset of the Civil War, the seminary was closed in June 1861, with sporadic reopenings occurring until October 1865, and the college's military equipment was donated to the Confederate army.

The school's library was destroyed by order of General T.K. Smith, Union army. In fact, by the end of the Civil War, only one of the school's buildings remained, and it was saved at the special request of General Sherman. Nearly ten years later, in 1874, an act of the Louisiana legislature established Louisiana State Agricultural and Mechanical College, implementing the Morrill Act of 1862, which designated the university as a land-grant college. In 1877, the present Louisiana State University emerged. Interim presidents led the university over the next six and half decades until 1941, when the second of this university's presidents with a military background was named.

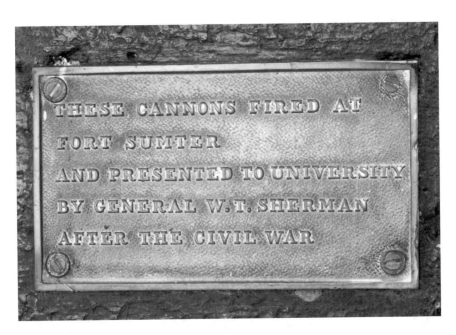

Plaque for the brass cannons. *Photo by Layne Photography.*

Major General Campbell Hodges served in this capacity from 1941 to 1944. He had been commandant of cadets at the U.S. Military Academy at West Point and a military adviser to President Hoover. From 1951 to 1961, Lieutenant General Troy Middleton served as the third LSU president with a military resume. He had been the recipient of the Distinguished Service Medal for his bravery in the Meuse-Argonne Offensive during World War I and later for his leadership during the Battle of the Bulge in World War II.

General William Tecumseh Sherman recalled many fond memories and experiences during his tenure as superintendent of the seminary and tried to shield the institution he had led from the aftermath of war as much as possible. One of his overt gestures of reconciliation involved the donation of these two cannons, captured from the Confederacy, to LSU after the end of the Civil War in 1886. There is a brass plaque that identifies them and reads as follows:

THESE CANNONS FIRED AT

FORT SUMTER

AND PRESENTED TO UNIVERSITY

BY GENERAL W.T. SHERMAN

AFTER THE CIVIL WAR

The two brass cannons were originally thought to be Ames Napoleon cannons when they were first donated and arrived on campus. Later, rifling was discovered in the muzzles, and that was unlike the Napoleon cannons, which were smoothbores. Eventually, it was also discovered that the tubes in these cannons were made in Springfield, Massachusetts, in 1861 by Nathan Peabody Ames of Ames Manufacturing Company and that they were fieldpieces with limited range. Charles T. James, who worked with Ames Manufacturing, had developed a rifled projectile and rifling system and produced 3.80-inch bore rifled cannons in at least six known variants. Collectively, these were all known as fourteen-pounder James Rifle cannons. The first five variants were bronze, while the final type was made of iron. The confusion that arose between the James Rifle cannon and the Ames Napoleon cannon might have occurred because the Federal army lacked rifled siege artillery and resorted to rifling its existing smoothbore pieces.

Over the years, speculation has run rampant that these were not the Confederate guns that fired on Fort Sumter and were later donated to LSU by General Sherman. Some pundits proposed the theory that this legend was almost certainly a fabricated myth started in the late nineteenth century. They further stated that it is highly possible that David F. Boyd, LSU's superintendent in 1870, acquired them as war surplus. While there is a suspicion that Boyd paid for them himself, he listed the cannons as gifts from a "friend of LSU," which is how he normally referred to Sherman. To add insult to injury, it is also speculated that the venerable cannons were actually acquired in 1909, long after Sherman and Boyd were both dead, to add to the decor of the Old State Capitol Building.

All of this notwithstanding, the state of Louisiana, the city of Baton Rouge and Louisiana State University seem to stand by the words on the brass plaque that adhere to the more romanticized account of the origins of the existence of the military cannons on campus. The thoughts and dreams of honor and chivalry existing between opposing sides following a bloody civil war, especially with one side winning such a lopsided victory, is particularly appealing. This description certainly appears to fit in better with the aura that envelops the Memorial Oak Grove on the LSU campus, where each of the thirty trees is dedicated to a fallen soldier who died while in service to the United States.

Appendix I

ORIGINS OF
BATON ROUGE'S NAME

There are various and diverse accounts regarding the origins of this city's name. Pierre Le Moyne Sieur d'Iberville wrote on March 17, 1699, that he and his expedition had reached a small stream at the right of the Mississippi River. There, not far from the bank and on a high bluff, they found a reddened maypole without branches that they called a red stick. About two hundred years later, Charles Étienne Arthur Gayarré, a noted Louisiana historian and grandson of Étienne de Boré, wrote a different account of the origin of the name. In his four-volume book on Louisiana history, Gayarré, who is commonly referred to as the father of Louisiana history, claims that the expedition came upon a gigantic cypress tree with a reddish tint on the east bank of the Mississippi River. Its ocre trunk, tall and straight, suggested a pole—a *baton rouge*, as the French called it—possibly marking and separating the hunting grounds of the Bayougoula (Bayagoula) and the Houma Indians for more than three hundred years. Over time, suggestions have been made that the Houma Indians used this pole for ceremonies, which incorporated hanging fish heads and animal skins on it, helping to produce the reddish tint.

Adding to the differences and variations between the names "red stick" and "red pole," there is some speculation that the name originated with the Choctaw Indian name for red pole: *iti humma*, or Istrouma. Presently, Istrouma is a well-known neighborhood in the city of Baton Rouge.

Appendix II

ORIGINS OF THE

AMERICAN DOLLAR SIGN

Oliver Pollock's accounting documents led Dr. James Alton James in his biography of Pollock to trace the origins of the American dollar sign directly to his records. The Spanish used the piaster as their equivalent for the American dollar notation, which was "dlls," "dls" or "ds." The mark for a Spanish piaster was a double shank "P" with an "S" at the upper right-hand corner. According to C. Ward Bond in his *Downtown Baton Rouge, a Story*, over the years Pollock superimposed the "S" on the double shank "P," which eventually he shortened to using only an "S" with a double line through it.

Appendix III

ORIGINS OF THE
NICKNAME "KINGFISH"

In 1932, about the time when Governor Huey P. Long was elected Louisiana's senator, he seemed to acquire a new nickname and began calling himself the "Kingfish." The name was supposedly taken from the character who led the Mystic Knights of the Sea in the popular radio comedy show *Amos 'n' Andy*. Somehow the name pleased Long, and he made no effort to discourage its use. The magazine *Vanity Fair*, however, saw it as a chance to ridicule him, saying that the Louisiana kingfish has a "big mouth, feeds off suckers, thrives best in mud and slime, and is very hard to catch."

In Huey Long's autobiography, *Every Man a King*, he gives a different version of how the name got started and then was applied to him. He stated that from time to time during heated political battles, he designated several political enemies as "Kingfish." An error in writing the state's highway bonds resulted in wording the most recent statute as stating that the highway bonds were to be sold by the Highway Commission instead of by the governor. When this was brought to his attention, Governor Long replied, "I am participating here anyway, gentlemen. For the present you can just call me the Kingfish."

The question remains, though: what happened to the statue of Hernando de Soto, the Spanish explorer who was the first European to cross the Mississippi River? There are some who say that when the reflecting pool was filled in 1960, the wrecking crew demolished the De Soto statue and dropped its remains in the Mississippi River. The *LSU Building Information Guide* proposes that the statue could have been tipped over into the pool before it was filled. The present director of Facility Development, Bill Eskew, stated that he had heard that pieces of the statue were chopped up and placed with other concrete rocks along the banks of the Mississippi to prevent erosion. Jason Soileau speculated that some remnants of the statue could still remain underground where the pool had once been. Others believe that the students toppled it, subsequently crushed it and then flung it into the mighty river. If this is true, then the statue met the same fate as the Spanish explorer. De Soto, as he was dying in the vicinity of present-day Ferriday, Mississippi, requested that he be "laid to rest" in the Mississippi River. Today, we know that all that remains of where the reflecting pool and the statue once stood are two lines of oak trees creating an alley.

Postscript: Restoring the Greek Amphitheater and surrounding area is an important part of the project "Enhancing the Core," which seeks to redesign and improve the center of the LSU campus. The Greek Amphitheater, like the Memorial Tower, is part of the original fabric of the campus and, as such, needs to be restored. There are many people connected with the university who recognize that it is a landmark in need of repairs and seek to get the funds necessary to do this. Hopefully, this can be accomplished in the near future.

BIBLIOGRAPHY

BOOKS

Armstrong, Annabelle M. *Historic Neighborhoods of Baton Rouge.* Charleston, SC: The History Press, 2010.

Bond, Ward C. *A Story of Downtown, 1963–2008.* Baton Rouge, LA: Chatsworth Press, 2008.

Bruns, Mrs. Thomas N. Carter. *Louisiana Portraits Bicentennial Edition.* New Orleans, LA: National Society of the Colonial Dames of America in the State of Louisiana, 1975.

Carleton, Mark T. *River Capitol: An Illustrated History of Baton Rouge.* Woodland Hills, CA: Windsor Publications, 1981.

Caughey, John Walton. *Bernardo de Gálvez in Louisiana, 1776–1783.* Gretna, LA: Pelican Publishing Company, 1998.

Davis, Edwin Adams. *Louisiana: A Narrative History.* 3rd ed. Baton Rouge, LA: Claitor's Publishing Division, 1971.

Fortier, Alceé. *A History of Louisiana.* Vol. 2, *The Spanish Domination and the Cession to the United States.* Edited by Jo Ann Carrigan. Baton Rouge, LA: Claitor's Publishing Division, 1972.

Gayarré, Charles E. *Romance of the History of Louisiana.* New York: D. Appleton & Company, 1848.

Haase, Carol K. *Louisiana's Old State Capitol.* Gretna, LA: Pelican Publishing Company, 2009.

Holmes, Jack D., PhD. *The 1779 "Marcha de Galvez": Louisiana's Giant Step Forward in the American Revolution.* Baton Rouge, LA: Baton Rouge Bicentennial Corporation, 1974.

King, Grace. *A History of Louisiana.* New Orleans, LA: Graham Publishing Company, 1905.

Krousel, Hilda S., PhD. *Don Antonio de Ulloa: First Spanish Governor to State of Louisiana.* Baton Rouge, LA: VAAPR Inc., 1981.

Kubly, Vincent F. *The Louisiana Capitol, Its Art and Architecture.* Gretna, LA: Pelican Publishing Company, 1995.

Long, Huey P. *Every Man a King.* Chicago: Quadrangle Paperbacks, 1933.

Meyers, Rose. *A History of Baton Rouge, 1699–1812.* Ann Arbor, MI: Louisiana State University Press, 1976.

Montero de Pedro, José, Marqués de Casa Mena. *The Spanish in New Orleans and Louisiana.* Translated by Richard E. Chandler. Gretna, LA: Pelican Publishing Company, 2000.

Sakai, Saburo, with Martin Caidin and Fred Saito. *Samurai.* Garden City, NY: Nelson Doubleday Inc., 1957.

Symonds, Craig L. *Historical Atlas of the U.S. Navy.* Annapolis, MD: Naval Institute Press, 2001.

White, Richard D. *Kingfish: The Reign of Huey P. Long.* New York: Random House, 2006.

Woodward, Ralph Lee, Jr. *Tribute to Don Bernardo de Gálvez.* Baton Rouge, LA: Historic New Orleans Collection, 1979.

NEWSPAPER ARTICLES

Baton Rouge Advocate. "Huey P. Long, from Traveling Salesman to the Governor's Mansion." June 29, 2009. Educational Services Department of the *Advocate.*

———. "Louisiana." Monday, June 29, 2009. Educational Services Department of the *Advocate.*

———. "Memorial Hall Governors." May 14, 2012. Educational Services Department of the *Advocate.*

———. "Oliver Pollock: Financier of the American Revolution." Monday, November 7, 2011. Educational Services Department of the *Advocate.*

———. "Wrought Iron Fence Old State Capitol." People Section, Wednesday, June 8, 2011.

Blitzer, Carol Anne. "The Pentagon Barracks." *Baton Rouge Advocate,* January 26, 1998.

Buchanan, Don. "Controversy Is Looming Over Fence at Old State Capitol." *State Times,* July 26, 1972.

Campbell, Cynthia. "Sex, Scandal, Assassination." *Baton Rouge Advocate,* May 17, 1992.

Cotton, George. "Red Stick Erected Again on Historic Scott's Bluff." *Sunday Advocate,* August 29, 1976.

De Mers, John. "The Boulevard's Naughty Lady." *Baton Rouge Advocate,* July 22, 1973.

Gueymard, Ernest. "If an Old Fence Could Talk." *State Times,* October 12, 1971.

———. "Iron Fence Battle Simmers." *State Times,* January 15, 1974.

———. "More Tales About Old Capitol." *State Times,* January 22, 1974.

Lazaro, Dan. "Monumentally, Baton Rouge." *Baton Rouge Advocate*, February 10, 1974.

Leger, Benjamin. "Relic in Ruins." *Daily Reveille*, January 30, 2003. Louisiana State University.

Meaur, Lindsey. "Enchanted Forest Finds Roots Deep in University History." *Daily Reveille*, December 2, 2009. Louisiana State University.

Morris, George. "Changes at the Ole War Skule." *Baton Rouge Advocate*, May 30, 1994.

New Orleans Times-Picayune. "Bond Sale Drive to Open Today." May 14, 1950.

———. "End of the Road for a Replica of the Liberty Bell." July 11, 1950.

———. "He Must Ring the Bell." Section 3, May 21, 1950.

———. "Replica of Original Liberty Bell, Cast in France." July 07, 1950.

———. "Testing the Liberty Bell Replica." May 25, 1950.

The People's Page. "Louisiana's Elusive Liberty Bell." Radiofone, July 1986.

Price, Ann. "Old State Capitol Nears Completion." *Baton Rouge Advocate*, October 24, 1993.

———. "On the Road with Huey." *Baton Rouge Advocate*, August 22, 1993.

Scroggs, William O., PhD. Address presented at meeting of Historical Society of East and West Baton Rouge. Printed in the *State Times*, May 16, 1932.

State Times. "Old Arsenal on National Register of Historic Places." July 4, 1973.

Stewart, Gwen. "Old State Capitol Slated for Return to Late 1800s." *State Times*, Tuesday, January 30, 1968.

Warr, Chante Dionne. "Gateway to History: Capitol Fence Rises Again." *Baton Rouge Advocate*, July 30, 2008.

INDEX

INDEX

INDEX

ABOUT THE AUTHOR

D r. Hilda S. Krousel was born Hilda Sánchez on October 8, 1927, in Tampa, Florida. There she attended Jefferson High School, graduating as salutatorian of her class in 1945. She then enrolled in Florida State College for Women (which became Florida State University in 1946) in Tallahassee, Florida, pursuing a Bachelor of Arts degree with a major in history. Graduating cum laude in 1949, she was selected for membership in the honorary societies of Phi Beta Kappa, Phi Kappa Phi and Phi Alpha Theta. The following semester, she enrolled again at Florida State University, this time in the program for graduate studies in the history department. In 1951, she was awarded a Master of Arts degree specializing in history, with a minor in Spanish literature.

In the fall of 1951, she received a graduate assistantship in the History Department at Louisiana State University in Baton Rouge, Louisiana. She pursued the program of studies there, seeking to earn the Doctor of Philosophy degree.

The PhD program of studies took a detour when she met and married Walter R. Krousel Jr. in 1953. Accepting a position as an editor with the

LSU Press, which permitted part-time enrollment at the university, she worked there until 1955. In 1956, the first of their five children was born. Presently, they have eight grandchildren and one great-grandson. In 1970, Louisiana State University conferred a Doctor of Philosophy degree on Hilda Sánchez Krousel.

In 1981, VAAPR Inc. published *Don Antonio de Ulloa: First Spanish Governor to the State of Louisiana* by Dr. Hilda Sánchez Krousel. In 2007, this book was translated into Spanish by John C. Cordero of Spring Valley, New York, and published in Madrid.

Dr. Krousel continues to live in Baton Rouge, Louisiana.